Mind Entwined

Unraveling the Mystery of Shared Psychotic Disorder

Well-Being Publishing

Although the author and publisher have made every effort to ensure that the information in this book was correct at press time, the author and publisher do not assume and hereby disclaim any liability to any party for any loss, damage, or disruption caused by errors or omissions, whether such errors or omissions result from negligence, accident, or any other cause.

This publication is designed to provide accurate and authoritative information with regard to the subject matter covered. It is sold with the understanding that the publisher is not engaged in rendering professional services. If legal advice or other expert assistance is required, the services of a competent professional should be sought.

The fact that an organization or website is referred to in this work as a citation and/or a potential source of further information does not mean that the author or the publisher endorses the information the organization or website may provide or recommendations it may make.

Please remember that Internet websites listed in this work may have changed or disappeared between when this work was written and when it is read.

Contents

Introduction

Shared psychotic disorder sits at an unusual intersection of intimacy, belief, and clinical uncertainty. It is not simply a matter of two people agreeing on the same unusual idea. What makes the condition distinctive is the way a delusional belief can move through a relationship, taking hold in a second person whose emotional dependence, isolation, or trust makes that belief feel increasingly real. In the clinical literature, the phenomenon has long been described as rare and difficult to define with precision, which helps explain why it has often been overlooked or folded into broader diagnostic categories [1].

The classic picture involves a close pair: a dominant or highly conviction-driven individual and a more receptive partner who begins to adopt the same false belief. Yet the relationship pattern can vary. The bond may be marital, familial, caregiving, or otherwise emotionally enmeshed, and the belief may spread through repeated conversation, shared routines, and mutual reinforcement. In some reported cases, the transmission has occurred even when the pair were not physically together, showing that proximity is not the only factor; sustained contact and relational influence can be enough to shape the shared reality [3].

For mental health professionals, the condition matters because it can be mistaken for stubbornness, cultural belief, personality conflict, or a primary psychotic disorder in both individuals. For caregivers and family members, it can be missed because the relationship itself may appear devoted, protective, or simply private. The delusional content may also be plausible on the surface—concerns about surveillance, persecution, poisoning, infidelity, or betrayal are common themes in reported cases—

making the underlying pathology harder to spot until functioning begins to deteriorate.

Another reason this disorder is so challenging is that the secondary person is not merely “copying” a belief in a casual sense. Adoption of the delusion usually unfolds in a context of emotional reliance and limited outside correction. The affected person may have few alternative relationships, little opportunity for reality testing, or a strong fear of losing the bond that anchors daily life. In that setting, disagreement can feel more threatening than agreement, and the shared belief can become part of the relationship’s emotional glue.

Modern psychiatry no longer treats the condition as a simple curiosity. It is recognized as a clinically meaningful phenomenon that requires careful assessment of both the content of the belief and the relationship in which it develops. At the same time, the literature continues to note ambiguity about boundaries, classification, and the best way to distinguish shared psychosis from related presentations [1]. That ambiguity is one reason a clear, practical understanding is so important: when the diagnosis is missed, the relationship pattern and the risk it creates may remain intact.

For that reason, the discussion that follows will focus not only on symptoms, but on the relational environment in which symptoms emerge. Shared psychotic disorder is best understood by looking at how conviction is reinforced, how dependency narrows perspective, and how a private reality can harden into something both people defend. The details matter, because in many cases the first visible problem is not a bizarre statement, but a relationship that has become so closed, so intense, and so self-sealing that outside reality can no longer get in.

CHAPTER 1

Chapter 1: Understanding Shared Psychotic Disorder

Before the clinical details can be separated into definition, history, diagnosis, and common misunderstandings, it helps to pause on the basic shape of the phenomenon itself. Shared psychotic disorder has long occupied an uncertain place in psychiatry because it does not always present as a single, neatly bounded illness; it emerges through relationships, context, and the gradual narrowing of reality between two people. That relational quality is what makes the condition both compelling and easy to overlook. The term folie à deux reflects a history of clinicians trying to name a pattern that appears rare, mutable, and often hidden in plain sight [1][6].

Core definition and historical background of folie à deux

The term folie à deux entered psychiatric language in the late nineteenth century through the work of Charles Lasègue and Jean-Pierre Falret, who used it to describe a striking clinical pattern: a delusional belief appearing to pass from one person to another within a close relationship [6]. Their original observations emphasized not just the content of the belief, but the relational setting in which it took root. The people involved were usually bound by emotional closeness, dependency, and relative isolation from outside influence. That early description still shapes the modern understanding of the disorder, even though the terminology and diagnostic framework have changed over time.

At its core, folie à deux refers to a shared psychotic process in which one person's delusional system is adopted, reinforced, or elaborated by another. The person who first develops the belief is often called the primary, inducer, or dominant person, while the person who comes to share it is described as secondary, induced, or recipient. This language is useful, but it can also oversimplify what is happening. The secondary person is not merely repeating words like an echo; the belief is usually shaped by trust, emotional reliance, repeated exposure, and a narrowed social world. In that sense, the "sharing" is psychological as much as it is interpersonal.

Historically, the syndrome was treated as a rare curiosity, but it attracted sustained clinical attention because it raised difficult questions about the boundaries between individual illness and relational influence. Early psychiatrists saw it as a distinct condition with recognizable features, yet later authors began to question how separate it truly was from other psychotic disorders, personality vulnerabilities, or family dynamics [1]. That debate has never fully disappeared. Some cases clearly involve one severely psychotic person influencing another; others are more complicated, with both individuals showing varying degrees of vulnerability, fixed belief, and impairment. The result is a concept that remains clinically useful even as its exact edges have stayed somewhat blurred.

As psychiatric classification systems evolved, the condition was gradually reframed rather than abandoned. Modern diagnostic manuals have tended to treat shared delusional phenomena as uncommon and often embedded within broader disorders rather than as a fully independent illness. This shift reflects a more cautious view of the diagnosis: clinicians are encouraged to look for the underlying psychosis, mood disorder, neurocognitive condition, or environmental pressure that may be driving the shared belief. In practice, the historical label survives because it captures something important that other diagnoses can miss—the way a delusion can become organized around a relationship and sustained by it.

That historical perspective also helps explain why the condition has so often been misread. The old descriptions emphasized pairs, but later reports have shown that shared delusional systems can involve families, caregiving relationships, and even small groups [8][9]. The classic "two-person" model is still the best-known form, yet the essential feature is not the number of people but the transmission of a fixed false belief within a tightly connected social unit. A shared delusion may spread gradually through conversation, imitation, fear, or repeated reassurance, and in some cases the belief can persist even when the original source is no longer present. Reports have even described transmission through mediated contact, such as telephone-based interaction, underscoring how relationship structure can matter as much as physical proximity [3].

Seen in this light, folie à deux is best understood as both a historical term and a clinical clue. It points to a pattern recognized for more than a century: delusional conviction taking shape in one person and then becoming stabilized in another through emotional dependence and restricted reality testing. The older literature was right to notice the interpersonal force of the phenomenon, even if later psychiatry became more cautious about treating it as a neatly separate disease entity [1][6]. For present-day clinicians and caregivers, the historical background matters because it reminds us that the disorder is not only about false belief. It is about the social conditions that allow a false belief to seem shared, protected, and increasingly difficult to question.

How shared delusions develop and spread within relationships

Shared delusions rarely appear all at once. More often, they emerge through repetition, emotional pressure, and a gradual narrowing of the relationship's shared reality. One person's conviction may begin as a tentative interpretation, a suspicion, or a way of making sense of fear, stress, or confusion. If the other person is emotionally dependent, isolated, or highly invested in preserving closeness, that interpretation can be absorbed before it is ever fully examined. The belief then gains force not because it is objectively convincing, but because it is embedded in a relationship that rewards agreement and discourages doubt.

The process often begins with asymmetry. One person, usually the more dominant or more psychologically unstable member of the pair, introduces the idea with certainty. The second person may initially hesitate, question, or remain only partly convinced. Yet uncertainty can be uncomfortable in a close relationship, especially when the bond depends on loyalty, caretaking, or fear of abandonment. In that setting, agreeing may feel safer than resisting. Over time, repeated exposure to the same explanation, combined with the emotional authority of the first person, can make the belief feel familiar and therefore plausible. Familiarity is not the same as truth, but in highly enmeshed relationships the two can start to blur.

Reinforcement plays a central role in this spread. Each time the shared belief is treated as fact, it becomes easier to maintain. A neutral event is reinterpreted as evidence, a coincidence becomes a sign, and ordinary ambiguity is folded into the delusional framework. The second person may begin to participate in this process without fully realizing it, offering confirmatory details, avoiding contradictory information, or seeking out material that seems to support the belief. Once this loop is established, the relationship itself becomes a closed system. Outside perspectives are dismissed, and internal agreement starts to function as a substitute for reality testing.

Isolation intensifies this dynamic. When a person has little contact with friends, relatives, coworkers, or professionals who might challenge the belief, the relationship loses corrective input. The two individuals may spend so much time together that they share not only experiences but interpretations, moods, and anxieties. In that environment, the delusion can become a kind of private language. It may be expressed through repeated conversations, coded references, rituals, or mutual vigilance. The more the pair withdraws from outside feedback, the more the belief can seem self-evident, because nothing remains to interrupt it.

Fear is another powerful carrier. Delusional systems often gain momentum when they offer an explanation for distress that feels coherent and emotionally satisfying. A threatening outside force, a hidden conspiracy, a contaminant, or a persecutor can provide a shape to diffuse anxiety. For the secondary person, accepting the belief may reduce immediate tension by giving the fear a clear target. This is one reason shared delusions can persist even when they are disruptive. The belief is not only false; it is also regulating. It organizes emotion, reduces uncertainty, and creates the illusion of control.

Power dynamics determine how easily the belief spreads and how firmly it stays in place. In some relationships, the primary person is overtly controlling, insisting on obedience or punishing disagreement. In others, the influence is subtler, built on dependency, caretaking, or a history of emotional submission. The secondary person may have learned that harmony requires agreement, or that challenging the dominant partner leads to conflict, withdrawal, or blame. In those cases, the delusion is reinforced not just by persuasion but by the relationship's emotional economy. Compliance becomes a way to preserve connection, even when it distorts perception.

Cultural meaning can also shape how a shared belief takes form and how quickly it is accepted. A delusional idea is more likely to spread when it borrows from existing fears, shared values, or community narratives that already feel recognizable [10]. This does not mean culture causes the disorder, but it can provide the language through which the belief is expressed and justified. Likewise, when the delusion is tied to a concrete bodily complaint, such as infestation or contamination, the belief may be easier to transmit because it attaches to sensations that are difficult to disprove [7]. In such cases, the relationship does not merely transmit an idea; it helps reinterpret ordinary experience until both people inhabit the same distorted explanation.

What makes the spread of shared delusion clinically significant is not only that two people come to believe the same falsehood, but that the belief becomes embedded in the structure of their bond. The relationship no longer simply contains the delusion; it sustains it. Agreement becomes a marker of loyalty, doubt becomes a threat, and reality itself is negotiated through emotional dependence. By the time the pattern is visible from the outside, the delusion may have already been reinforced by months or years of mutual adaptation.

Diagnostic context: where the condition fits in contemporary psychiatry

In contemporary psychiatry, shared psychotic disorder is best understood as a descriptive clinical phenomenon rather than a fixed, self-contained disease category. Its placement has shifted over time because the condition does not always behave like a classic primary psychotic disorder. The central feature is not merely that two people hold the same unusual belief, but that one person's delusional framework develops in close relational contact with another person who becomes increasingly persuaded by it. That relational transmission is what makes the diagnosis clinically distinctive, and also what makes it difficult to fit neatly into modern classification systems [1][6].

Historically, the diagnosis appeared in older nosologies under labels such as folie à deux, and traces of that framework remain in international classification systems. At the same time, modern psychiatry has become more cautious about treating it as a stand-alone explanation. Reviews of the literature have noted continuing uncertainty about the essence and boundaries of the syndrome, including whether it should be understood as its own disorder, a specifier, or a relational expression of another psychotic illness [1]. This uncertainty matters in practice because the clinician must decide whether the shared belief represents a discrete syndrome, a manifestation of an underlying condition, or both.

That question is especially important because the person who first develops the delusional belief is often not the same person as the one who later adopts it. In many cases, the initiating individual has a primary psychotic disorder, severe mood disorder with psychotic features, delusional disorder, or another psychiatric condition that supplies the original delusional content. The second person may have no prior psychotic history and may appear more psychologically vulnerable, suggestible, dependent, or socially isolated. In such situations, the shared belief is not the most complete diagnosis; it is a relational pattern that can occur alongside another mental illness in one or both people [9][2][4].

For that reason, contemporary assessment usually begins with a broader diagnostic frame. The clinician asks not only whether a delusion is present, but also how it arose, who first expressed it, how it is maintained, and what happens when the two individuals are separated. Separation has long been a useful clinical test because shared beliefs may weaken when the interpersonal reinforcement is reduced, although not every case resolves cleanly in that way. The diagnostic picture can also be complicated by the fact that the secondary person may display partial insight, fluctuating conviction, or symptoms that are shaped by anxiety, trauma, or a preexisting personality style rather than by a primary psychotic process alone [1][4].

This is one reason shared psychotic disorder is often discussed alongside other psychotic and delusional conditions rather than as an isolated entity. In practice, differential diagnosis must consider delusional disorder, schizophrenia spectrum disorders, mood disorders with psychotic features, substance-induced psychosis, medical causes of psychosis, and culturally shaped belief systems that are unusual but not pathological. The diagnostic task is not to label every odd belief as shared psychosis; it is to determine whether the belief is fixed, false, impairing, and sustained through a close relationship in a way that exceeds ordinary influence or persuasion. Case literature on delusional infestation, for example, shows how shared conviction can appear in a specific thematic form while still requiring careful exclusion of medical and psychiatric alternatives [5][7][8].

The contemporary view also emphasizes that the diagnosis has practical value even if its boundaries remain debated. Naming the phenomenon can help clinicians recognize relational dynamics that might otherwise be missed, especially in family systems, caregiving arrangements, or highly isolated partnerships. It alerts providers to the possibility that treating only one individual may be insufficient if the shared belief is being continuously reinforced by the relationship itself. In that sense, the diagnosis functions as a clinical lens: it directs attention to interpersonal transmission, dependency, and reinforcement, while leaving room for the broader psychiatric formulation that each person may require [6][9][2].

There is also an important caution built into this modern framing. Because the condition is rare and its borders are not sharply defined, it can be overcalled when clinicians encounter disagreement, unusual religious or cultural ideas, or intense family loyalty. Conversely, it can be missed when a secondary person seems merely anxious, compliant, or confused rather than overtly psychotic. The best contemporary practice is therefore not to search for a label in isolation, but to evaluate the belief within its relational, developmental, and clinical context. Shared psychotic disorder fits psychiatry today as a reminder that psychosis is not always contained within one mind; sometimes it is sustained, shaped, and amplified between minds [1][10][3].

Common misconceptions and why the disorder is frequently missed

One reason shared psychotic disorder is missed so often is that it can hide behind ordinary relational behavior. A close pair may seem intensely loyal, private, or simply "in sync," especially if they have spent long periods together and rely on each other for emotional stability. From the outside, the bond may appear unusual but not necessarily pathological. Even when the beliefs involved are clearly false, the interpersonal context can make them look like a shared coping style rather than a psychiatric problem. Clinicians and family members may therefore focus on the content of the belief and overlook the more important question of how the belief is being maintained between people.

A second misunderstanding is the assumption that both people must be equally ill. In reality, one person is usually more psychologically dominant, more convinced, or more impaired, while the other may be more suggestible, dependent, or fearful of separation. This asymmetry matters because the secondary person may not present as overtly psychotic in the usual sense. They may seem anxious, guarded, or preoccupied, but still able to function in many areas of life. That partial preservation of functioning can delay recognition, especially when the person does not volunteer the delusional content directly or frames it as a reasonable concern rather than a fixed belief. Reviews of the literature have also emphasized that the condition remains difficult to define cleanly, which contributes to inconsistent recognition in practice [1].

Another common error is treating the shared belief as evidence of a shared external reality. When two people describe the same unlikely event, they may be taken at face value if their story is coherent, emotionally compelling, or reinforced by anxiety. This is particularly true when the belief is embedded in a real-life stressor: a health complaint, a family conflict, a perceived threat, or a social dispute. In those situations, the delusional material can sound like an exaggerated interpretation of something plausible. The clinical challenge is that the belief often grows out of a recognizable concern, then becomes increasingly rigid, elaborate, and resistant to correction. Conditions such as delusional infestation illustrate how fixed false beliefs can persist despite the absence of supporting evidence, making the line between worry and delusion easy to miss when the presentation is filtered through another person's influence [5].

Shared psychosis is also frequently overlooked because the secondary person may appear to improve or become less convinced in settings where the primary relationship is absent. That fluctuation can be mistaken for ambivalence, manipulation, or simple inconsistency. In fact, it may reflect how dependent the belief is on the relationship itself. Once the pair is separated, the emotional pressure that sustained the delusion may weaken, and the secondary person may regain more reality testing. If a clinician sees only the separated individual, the earlier shared pattern may never emerge. This is one reason collateral information is so important; without it, the case can be misclassified as a standalone delusional disorder, anxiety condition, or even a personality issue.

Cultural context can further complicate recognition. Not every unusual belief is delusional, and not every intense conviction signals psychosis. Some ideas are shaped by religion, community norms, family narratives, or culturally accepted explanations for suffering. When clinicians are unfamiliar with that background, they may pathologize beliefs that are shared and meaningful within a broader social framework. The opposite error also occurs: a genuinely delusional belief may be dismissed as cultural difference, especially if it is expressed in a way that sounds familiar or is supported by a small, insular group. Careful assessment requires attention to whether the belief is fixed, false, and resistant to correction, rather than simply unusual or culturally specific.

The disorder is also missed because it is often discovered only after a crisis. A family may seek help when there is aggression, self-neglect, legal conflict, medical overuse, or a sudden breakdown in functioning. Until then, the pair may have adapted around the delusion in ways that conceal its severity. They may avoid certain topics, limit contact with outsiders, or build daily routines around the belief. In some cases, the secondary person presents first with a physical complaint, distress, or anxiety, while the shared delusion remains hidden behind the more visible symptom. Case reports have shown that even when the delusional content is medically implausible, the initial presentation may be routed through emergency or general medical settings rather than psychiatry [7][4].

Finally, the condition is missed because it does not always fit neatly into the diagnostic habits of modern practice. Clinicians are trained to identify individual symptom clusters, but shared psychosis is relational by nature. It asks the evaluator to think about influence, dependency, isolation, and interpersonal reinforcement, not just symptom checklists. If the assessment stops at the level of the individual, the shared structure of the problem can remain invisible. That is why the diagnosis is often delayed, debated, or replaced by other labels until the relational pattern becomes unmistakable. The literature has repeatedly noted this ambiguity, including cases in family settings where close contact and isolation made transmission easier to sustain [9][2].

CHAPTER 2

Chapter 2: The Psychology Behind Shared Belief

To understand why a shared belief becomes so compelling, it is necessary to look beyond the content of the belief itself and examine the relationship that carries it. In shared psychotic disorder, the psychological force is rarely a single factor; it is usually a convergence of emotional reliance, repeated interpersonal signaling, and a narrowed field of reality in which outside correction loses its influence. The bond between the people involved can make certain ideas feel safer, more coherent, or less threatening than uncertainty, especially when the relationship has become the main source of stability.

Attachment, dependency, and emotional enmeshment

Attachment is one of the most important pathways through which a shared belief can become emotionally protected. In many cases, the relationship is not merely close; it is organized around one person's need for safety, direction, or reassurance and the other person's role as the source of that security. When attachment becomes highly dependent, disagreement can feel less like a difference of opinion and more like a threat to the bond itself. The secondary person may learn, often without consciously deciding to do so, that preserving connection matters more than testing reality. In that setting, a delusional idea can be received not as an odd claim to be examined, but as part of the emotional contract that holds the relationship together.

Dependency intensifies this process because it reduces the psychological room needed for independent judgment. A person who relies on another for housing, finances, daily structure, emotional regulation, or protection may become deeply invested in maintaining harmony. The more fragile the surrounding life circumstances, the more costly it can feel to question the dominant person's beliefs. Even ordinary uncertainty may be experienced as dangerous if it risks conflict, abandonment, or loss of support. Over time, the dependent person may begin to monitor their own reactions, suppress doubts, and adapt their interpretations to match the other person's certainty. What begins as accommodation can gradually become internalized belief.

This is especially likely when attachment insecurity is already present. People who fear rejection, abandonment, or relational rupture may become highly responsive to cues from a trusted figure, even when those cues are distorted. They may treat the other person's confidence as evidence, especially if their own confidence in judgment has been weakened by stress, trauma, or repeated invalidation. In such relationships, the delusional belief may function like a stabilizer: it offers a shared explanation, a shared enemy, or a shared sense of purpose. The belief can reduce ambiguity in the short term, which helps explain why it may feel emotionally compelling even when it is objectively implausible.

Emotional enmeshment deepens the problem by blurring the boundary between one person's inner world and the other's. In an enmeshed relationship, feelings, fears, and interpretations are treated as if they belong to both people at once. There may be little tolerance for difference, privacy, or separate perspective. The pair can begin to operate as a closed system in which each person's emotional state continually reinforces the other's. When one person becomes anxious, suspicious, or preoccupied, the other may absorb that state rather than evaluate it. Repeated exposure to the same fear-laden narrative can then make the belief feel familiar, and familiarity is often mistaken for truth.

Clinical descriptions of shared psychotic disorder repeatedly note the importance of close, isolated relationships in which one person's delusions are transmitted to another [1][9][4]. That transmission is rarely a simple act of persuasion. It is more often a process of emotional alignment shaped by trust, repetition, and narrowed social contact. A person who has few outside relationships may have little opportunity to compare the shared narrative with alternative viewpoints. If the bond is also organized around caretaking or authority, questioning the belief may feel like disloyalty or defiance. The result is not just agreement, but a relationship structure that rewards conformity and punishes independent reality testing.

It is also important to recognize that dependency and enmeshment do not always look pathological from the inside. A person may describe their connection as devotion, loyalty, or mutual protection. In some families or partnerships, intense mutual reliance is normalized, especially when life has been marked by hardship, illness, or social marginalization. The clinical concern emerges when that closeness becomes rigid enough to exclude correction, outside contact, and personal differentiation. At that point, the relationship no longer serves as a buffer against distress; it becomes the very channel through which distorted belief is maintained. The secondary person is not simply convinced by an idea. They are being held inside a relational field where doubting the idea feels equivalent to risking the attachment itself.

For this reason, assessment of shared belief must always look beyond the content of the delusion and into the emotional architecture that sustains it. The key questions are often relational: Who depends on whom? Who sets the emotional tone? What happens when one person disagrees? How much room exists for separate relationships, separate opinions, and separate reality testing? When attachment is fused with dependency and enmeshment, the answer to those questions can explain why an implausible belief persists long after ordinary reassurance has failed. The belief is being protected not only by conviction, but by the fear of losing the relationship that conviction seems to secure.

Suggestibility, reinforcement, and confirmation loops

Suggestibility is not the same as gullibility. In shared psychotic disorder, it is often a heightened readiness to treat another person's perception as more reliable than one's own. That readiness tends to grow in relationships where trust, dependency, fear, or admiration already shape how reality is interpreted. A statement made with confidence, especially by the more dominant or emotionally central person, can begin to function like evidence. Over time, repeated exposure to the same claim lowers the threshold for acceptance, not because the belief has been logically proven, but because it has become familiar, emotionally charged, and socially reinforced.

This is one reason the disorder can develop so gradually. The secondary person may not adopt a delusion in a single dramatic moment. Instead, they may move through a series of small accommodations: first entertaining the idea, then refraining from challenging it, then interpreting ambiguous events through its lens. Each step makes the next one easier. Once a person begins to organize experience around the shared belief, suggestibility increases further because the mind starts selecting information that fits the dominant narrative. What was once uncertain begins to feel increasingly obvious simply through repetition and emotional rehearsal.

Reinforcement plays a central role in this process. When a belief is met with agreement, alarm, or protective behavior, it gains interpersonal weight. If the primary person reacts to neutral events as if they confirm the delusion, the secondary person receives a constant stream of cues that the belief deserves attention. Even ordinary behaviors can become reinforcing: checking locks, avoiding certain neighbors, changing routines, or scanning for signs of danger. These actions do not merely respond to the belief; they help organize daily life around it, making the belief feel practical and therefore more credible. In this way, behavior becomes a kind of proof, even when no objective evidence exists.

Confirmation loops form when the relationship begins to filter experience in a closed circuit. The belief leads to selective attention; selective attention produces selective interpretation; selective interpretation then appears to confirm the belief. A minor coincidence is noticed, remembered, and discussed. Contradictory information is dismissed as ignorance, hostility, or part of the threat itself. The more the pair relies on each other for interpretation, the less room remains for corrective feedback. In severe cases, the loop becomes self-sealing: the absence of evidence is treated as evidence of a cover-up, and the failure to find confirmation only deepens suspicion.

These loops are especially powerful when the people involved share isolation, stress, or a narrow social world. Without outside voices to interrupt the pattern, the relationship becomes its own reality-testing system. The primary person may set the interpretive tone, but the secondary person often helps sustain it by asking questions that assume the belief is true, by seeking reassurance in ways that intensify vigilance, or by avoiding conversations that might create conflict. The result is not simply passive imitation. It is a reciprocal process in which fear, attention, and repeated validation gradually harden a fragile idea into a seemingly stable certainty. Case reports have described this kind of transmission in close family and partner relationships, including situations in which the shared belief was maintained through sustained contact and mutual reinforcement [9][2][4].

Clinically, this matters because the content of the delusion may be less important than the mechanism that sustains it. A belief about infestation, surveillance, poisoning, or persecution can become entrenched through the same psychological pathway if the relationship rewards vigilance and discourages doubt. Studies and case reports on shared delusional states repeatedly show that close contact, emotional dependence, and limited external reality checks are common features of these presentations [1][6][8]. The specific theme may change, but the process remains recognizably similar: one person introduces or intensifies a conviction, the other becomes more receptive through attachment or stress, and the pair's shared interpretations begin to function as their primary source of truth.

Understanding suggestibility, reinforcement, and confirmation loops is important because it shifts attention from the question of whether a belief is "strange enough" to the question of how it is being maintained. Shared psychotic disorder is not sustained by delusion alone. It is sustained by a relational environment that repeatedly rewards belief and penalizes skepticism. When that environment changes, the loop can weaken; when it remains intact, even implausible ideas can feel increasingly self-evident to both people involved.

Stress, isolation, and vulnerability to distorted beliefs

Stress can make a belief feel less like an idea and more like a lifeline. When people are under sustained pressure, the mind often becomes more selective about what it can tolerate: uncertainty feels harder to bear, ambiguous events seem more threatening, and explanations that offer immediate coherence can gain unusual force. In that state, a distorted belief may function as an organizing principle. It reduces confusion, gives shape to fear, and creates the sense that something specific is happening rather than nothing making sense at all. For a person already vulnerable through anxiety, grief, trauma, or psychiatric symptoms, the appeal of a fixed explanation can be especially strong because it offers relief from mental chaos, even when that explanation is clearly false.

That relief is part of what makes stress so important in shared psychotic disorder. The belief does not have to be persuasive in a logical sense; it only has to feel stabilizing enough to survive scrutiny. Under chronic stress, people are more likely to rely on familiar sources of interpretation and less likely to test assumptions against broader reality. Small signs are noticed, remembered, and linked together into a pattern. Neutral events are read as meaningful. Once a relationship has become the main channel through which reality is filtered, the two people may begin to reinforce each other's interpretations without recognizing how narrowed that process has become. The result is not simply agreement, but a mutual reduction in the capacity to consider alternative explanations.

Isolation intensifies this process by removing correctives. When a person has little contact with friends, relatives, coworkers, or other outside observers, there are fewer opportunities for ordinary reality testing. A strange concern that might have been questioned in a broader social setting can instead circulate repeatedly within the relationship, gaining familiarity through repetition. If the pair lives, travels, or makes decisions together in near-total privacy, the same story may be heard, retold, and elaborated until it begins to feel self-evident. In that environment, the absence of contradiction can be mistaken for confirmation. The belief is not necessarily becoming stronger because it is more true; it is becoming stronger because it is less exposed to challenge.

Isolation also changes the emotional meaning of doubt. In a highly closed relationship, disagreement may carry the threat of abandonment, conflict, or loss of the only reliable source of support. That makes it harder for the secondary person to question the dominant person's interpretation, even when part of them senses that something is off. Doubt can be experienced as disloyalty, fear, or betrayal rather than as a healthy sign of independent thought. Over time, the person may learn to suppress hesitation in order to preserve closeness. This is one reason shared delusions can appear so resilient: they are protected not only by conviction, but by the emotional cost of stepping outside the shared frame.

Stress and isolation are especially potent when they combine with vulnerability. A person who is already fatigued, grieving, depressed, socially dependent, cognitively overwhelmed, or recovering from a prior psychiatric episode may have less psychological reserve for evaluating unusual claims. In some cases, the stressor is external and obvious, such as financial hardship, illness, migration, domestic instability, or caregiving burden. In others, the strain is more subtle, accumulating through long periods of emotional deprivation or dependence. Research has noted that the transmission of delusional beliefs is shaped not only by symptom severity, but also by social and cultural context, which can either constrain or amplify the shared framework [10].

What makes vulnerability clinically significant is not that stress automatically causes delusion. Many people experience severe stress without losing contact with reality. The issue is that stress can lower resistance to distorted beliefs when other protective factors are weak. Good sleep, varied relationships, stable routines, access to reality-based feedback, and a sense of personal agency all help keep perception flexible. When those supports disappear, the mind may become more rigid and more dependent on whatever interpretation seems to reduce distress fastest. In a shared psychotic pattern, that interpretation is often supplied by the other person, whose confidence can substitute for evidence and whose emotional intensity can make the belief feel urgent.

This is why clinicians pay close attention to the surrounding conditions, not just the content of the belief. A bizarre idea expressed in a person who is isolated, frightened, and emotionally enmeshed is more concerning than the same idea mentioned casually in a well-supported social network. Stress narrows attention; isolation removes correction;

vulnerability makes acceptance easier. Together, they create a setting in which distorted beliefs can seem not only plausible, but necessary for survival.

Power dynamics, coercion, and the role of dominance

Power in shared psychotic disorder is rarely expressed as overt force alone. More often, it appears as a pattern of control over interpretation: who gets to define what is happening, whose fear counts as evidence, and which explanations are allowed to survive. In that sense, dominance is not only a matter of personality style but of epistemic authority—the authority to name reality. The dominant person may speak with certainty, dismiss doubt as weakness, and present their own perceptions as the only trustworthy account. Over time, the secondary person may come to rely on that account not because it is persuasive in a neutral sense, but because disagreement carries relational costs.

Coercion in these relationships can be subtle enough to be missed by outsiders. It may take the form of repeated correction, emotional withdrawal, threats of abandonment, ridicule, or the implication that safety depends on compliance. A person who questions the shared belief may be told they are disloyal, naive, unstable, or unable to see what is "obvious." This kind of pressure can narrow the secondary person's room for independent judgment. The issue is not simply that one person is more confident than the other; it is that confidence becomes a tool for shaping what the other person is permitted to think, say, or notice. In a number of reported cases, the shared belief develops in the context of close, insular relationships where external feedback is limited and the more dominant person's view becomes increasingly difficult to challenge [9][2].

Dominance also matters because it can determine who absorbs uncertainty and who exports it. In some pairs, the primary person actively organizes the environment around the delusion, while the secondary person adapts in order to preserve attachment or avoid conflict. This adaptation may look like agreement, but clinically it often reflects a survival strategy. The secondary person may remain outwardly compliant while privately doubting, or may gradually lose access to doubt altogether as repeated pressure redefines hesitation as danger. When the relationship is highly dependent, the cost of disagreement can feel larger than the cost of accepting an implausible explanation. That asymmetry is one reason shared beliefs can become so resistant to correction.

The role of dominance is especially important in relationships where one person controls access to information, social contact, money, transportation, or care. Isolation does not have to be absolute to be effective; it only needs to be sufficient to reduce competing perspectives. If the dominant person filters conversations, interprets events for both parties, or discourages outside consultation, the secondary person has fewer opportunities to reality-test the belief against broader social feedback. This is one reason shared delusions are often described in close dyads or family settings, where proximity and dependency create a closed loop of reinforcement [1][6]. In such settings, the relationship itself can become the main environment in which reality is negotiated.

It is also important to distinguish dominance from simple leadership or caregiving. Not every influential person in a close relationship is coercive, and not every dependent person is being controlled. What makes dominance clinically relevant is the pattern of diminishing autonomy. A healthy relationship allows disagreement without punishment, preserves access to outside input, and tolerates uncertainty. A coercive one increasingly punishes doubt and rewards submission. In shared psychotic disorder, that distinction matters because the shared belief is often sustained less by the content of the delusion than by the interpersonal structure that protects it. The more one person's authority is used to override the other's judgment, the more the relationship can function as a closed system.

Clinicians should pay attention to language that signals this imbalance. Phrases such as "I had to agree," "there was no point arguing," "they know better than everyone else," or "I stopped talking to anyone else about it" may indicate that the belief is being maintained through relational pressure rather than mutual conviction. The presence of fear, appeasement, or chronic self-doubt in the secondary person can be as telling as the bizarre belief itself. In some cases, the dominant person may not appear obviously psychotic at first glance, yet their interpersonal style is rigid, controlling, and intolerant of contradiction. That combination can make the delusional system feel organized and convincing, even when it is deeply detached from reality [4].

For assessment purposes, the question is not only whether a delusion is shared, but how the sharing is sustained. Who initiates the explanation? Who resists alternative interpretations? Who becomes anxious when outsiders are involved? Who is allowed to question the story without retaliation? These are not peripheral details; they are central to understanding how power keeps the belief alive. In many cases, the path out of the shared system begins when the secondary person regains enough psychological or practical independence to test their own perceptions again. Until then, dominance and coercion can make a false belief feel less like a belief than a rule for staying connected.

CHAPTER 3

Chapter 3: Signs, Symptoms, and Red Flags

At this stage, the question is no longer whether a belief is unusual, but whether it is beginning to reshape perception, behavior, and the shared life of the relationship. The warning signs of shared psychotic disorder are often subtle at first, especially because they can look like loyalty, concern, or simply an intense private bond. What matters clinically is the pattern that emerges when conviction starts to override reflection and when the relationship itself begins to organize what each person notices, fears, and accepts as real. The signs do not always announce themselves in dramatic fashion; more often, they appear as small but persistent shifts that narrow judgment and reduce contact with corrective feedback.

Behavioral and emotional warning signs in the primary and secondary person

The behavioral warning signs in the primary person often begin with a tightening of thought and conduct around the shared belief. The person may become increasingly preoccupied, repetitive, or argumentative, returning again and again to the same interpretation even when evidence does not support it. Daily routines may start to reorganize around the belief: checking, monitoring, avoiding, confronting, documenting, or seeking reassurance in ways that feel urgent and difficult to interrupt. What stands out clinically is not only the presence of an unusual idea, but the degree to which it begins to govern attention, conversation, and decision-making. In some cases, the person may appear more energized and certain than distressed; in others, they may become irritable, suspicious, or defensive whenever the belief is questioned. That defensiveness can be especially important, because it often signals that the belief has moved from a passing concern to a protected part of the person's identity or sense of control.

As the condition intensifies, the primary person may show a narrowing of social and emotional flexibility. They may withdraw from people who disagree, reject professional input, or reinterpret neutral feedback as proof of hostility, betrayal, or incompetence. Everyday events can be filtered through the delusional framework, so that ordinary delays, bodily sensations, or interpersonal conflicts are treated as confirmation. This pattern is not simply stubbornness. It reflects a reduction in reality testing, where the person's confidence in the belief begins to outweigh their ability to compare it with alternative explanations. In some presentations, the primary person may also display a heightened need to recruit others into the same interpretation, not only for validation but because agreement helps stabilize the belief. That effort to enlist the secondary person can look like persuasion, concern, or protection, even when it is functioning as a mechanism of reinforcement.

Emotionally, the primary person may oscillate between certainty and vulnerability. Fear is common, but it may be masked by anger, moral outrage, or a sense of mission. The person may feel uniquely aware, chosen, targeted, or responsible for uncovering a hidden threat. Such emotional states can make the belief feel less like a symptom and more like a duty. When the primary person experiences the belief as self-evident, they may become impatient with ambiguity and intolerant of any response that introduces doubt. This can create an escalating interpersonal pattern: the more others question the belief, the more the primary person feels misunderstood; the more misunderstood they feel, the more firmly they cling to the idea. In practice, this can make conversations increasingly circular and difficult to redirect.

The secondary person often shows a different but related set of warning signs. At first, the change may be subtle: hesitancy, increased deference, repeated checking with the primary person, or a growing tendency to adopt their language and assumptions. Over time, the secondary person may begin to mirror the primary person's fear, preoccupation, or certainty, even when their own earlier reactions were more tentative. This is often accompanied by a gradual weakening of independent judgment. The secondary person may stop comparing the shared belief with outside information, avoid making decisions without the primary person's input, or feel unable to trust their own perceptions. In many cases, the shift is visible in how quickly they accept the dominant explanation and how strongly they defend it once challenged. The belief may seem to "fit" because it offers emotional coherence, not because it has been critically examined.

Behaviorally, the secondary person may become increasingly aligned with the primary person's routines and restrictions. They may avoid certain places, people, or activities because the belief has made those settings feel unsafe or contaminated. They may change sleep patterns, spending habits, communication style, or household practices to accommodate the shared fear. This alignment can be mistaken for loyalty or empathy, but clinically it may indicate the erosion of a separate perspective. The secondary person may also show signs of internal conflict that are easy to overlook: nervous laughter, uncertainty, quiet questioning, or a brief moment of doubt followed by rapid retraction. These moments matter, because they can indicate that the belief is being maintained less by conviction alone than by relational pressure, dependency, or fear of rupture.

Emotionally, the secondary person may appear anxious, subdued, guilty, or increasingly dependent. Some become more passive, deferring to the primary person's interpretation to avoid conflict or preserve closeness. Others become more distressed than the primary person, especially if they are caught between lingering doubt and the need to remain aligned with the relationship. Shame can also emerge, particularly when the secondary person senses that something is not quite right but feels unable to name it. In some cases, the person may present with somatic complaints, sleep disruption, or generalized agitation that reflects the strain of maintaining a belief they have not fully made their own. The key clinical point is that the secondary person's symptoms may be less dramatic than the primary person's, but they are often deeply connected to the emotional cost of participation.

What makes these warning signs especially important is the way they interact. The primary person's certainty can create a psychological environment in which the secondary person's doubt feels unsafe, disloyal, or overwhelming. In turn, the secondary person's compliance can strengthen the primary person's conviction, making the belief appear shared, validated, and therefore more real. This mutual reinforcement can produce a closed system in which both people appear to be moving toward the same conclusion, while in fact one person is organizing the interpretive frame and the other is adapting to it. When that pattern appears, clinicians and caregivers should pay close attention not only to what each person believes, but to how each person behaves when questioned, corrected, or separated from the other. The warning signs are often clearest when the relationship itself is under strain and the shared belief becomes harder to sustain without constant reassurance [1][9][4].

Changes in reality testing, judgment, and daily functioning

Changes in reality testing are often among the earliest signs that a shared delusion is no longer confined to belief but is beginning to alter perception itself. Reality testing is the capacity to compare an internal interpretation with external evidence and to revise that interpretation when the facts do not fit. In shared psychotic disorder, this capacity does not usually disappear all at once. It erodes unevenly. A person may still function well in some areas of life while becoming increasingly unable to question one specific idea, especially if that idea is reinforced by a trusted partner or family member. Over time, ordinary uncertainty can be replaced by certainty that feels self-evident, even when it rests on weak or distorted evidence.

Clinically, this shift often shows up as a narrowing of what counts as proof. Ambiguous events are reclassified as meaningful signals, neutral interactions are treated as confirmation, and contradictions are dismissed as deception, ignorance, or hostility. The person may begin to rely less on direct observation and more on interpretation filtered through the shared belief. A missed phone call becomes suspicious. A stranger's glance becomes a warning. A routine sound in the house becomes evidence of intrusion, surveillance, or plotting. The more the belief is repeated within the relationship, the less room there is for alternative explanations to be considered fairly.

Judgment is affected in a related but distinct way. Once a shared belief becomes organizing, decisions are no longer made primarily on the basis of practicality, safety, or proportion. Instead, choices are shaped by the demands of the delusional framework. A person may stop answering calls, avoid neighbors, discard medication, refuse needed appointments, or spend money on measures meant to address the imagined threat. In some cases, the secondary person mirrors these choices even when they previously would have resisted them, because the relationship has become the main source of orientation and the cost of disagreement feels too high. This pattern has been described in case literature as unfolding within a family dynamic that continues to sustain the delusion rather than interrupt it [11].

Daily functioning often declines in small, cumulative ways before it becomes obviously impaired. Sleep may be disrupted by checking behaviors, fear, or prolonged conversations about the belief. Work performance can suffer because attention is repeatedly pulled toward monitoring, rumination, or avoidance. Household routines may become organized around the perceived threat, with time spent sealing windows, reviewing messages, hiding items, or rehearsing responses to imagined harm. Social life tends to shrink as well. Friends, relatives, clinicians, or coworkers may be avoided because they challenge the shared reality, and their questions can feel intrusive or dangerous. What begins as vigilance gradually becomes a way of life.

One reason these changes can be missed is that they may look, from the inside, like caution or loyalty rather than impairment. A person may insist they are simply "being careful" or "protecting the relationship," and in a narrow sense that may even seem true. The problem is not only the unusual belief itself, but the extent to which it begins to govern ordinary functioning. When a person cannot separate routine events from the alleged threat, cannot weigh evidence flexibly, or cannot make decisions without first consulting the delusional framework, reality testing is no longer serving its stabilizing role. The world becomes organized around a single interpretation, and everything else is forced to fit.

In the secondary person, this deterioration may be especially subtle. The individual may not appear overtly psychotic and may retain insight in other areas of life, yet still defer to the dominant person's version of events in ways that steadily weaken independent judgment. They may begin by agreeing "just to keep the peace," then gradually speak and act as though the belief were their own. At that point, the difference between endorsement and conviction can blur. The person may no longer know where personal observation ends and borrowed certainty begins, which makes daily functioning dependent on the relationship itself. The more isolated and emotionally bound the pair becomes, the harder it is for external reality to re-enter the system in a meaningful way.

For that reason, clinicians and caregivers often look less for dramatic psychotic behavior than for the practical consequences of a closed belief system. If a person's ability to work, parent, sleep, maintain hygiene, manage money, or interact safely is being reorganized around a fixed and implausible idea, the concern is not merely that the idea is unusual. It is that the person's judgment is no longer reliably anchored to shared reality, and the effects are beginning to spread into everyday life.

Relationship patterns that signal escalating risk

Relationship patterns that signal escalating risk are usually less about a single dramatic incident than about a gradual tightening of the interpersonal system. The bond begins to close in on itself. Outside perspectives are treated as interruptions, disagreement starts to feel like betrayal, and ordinary uncertainty is replaced by a shared urgency to explain, defend, or act on the belief. In clinical settings, this narrowing often appears before the delusion becomes fully fixed. The pair may spend increasing amounts of time together, reduce contact with friends or relatives, and rely more heavily on each other for interpretation of events. What once looked like closeness can become a sealed feedback loop, especially when the relationship already contains dependency or imbalance.

One of the clearest warning patterns is increasing exclusivity. The relationship becomes the primary, and sometimes the only, source of emotional validation. Decisions are made together, but not in a healthy collaborative sense; rather, one person's view becomes the default lens through which both people interpret reality. Questions from outsiders are brushed aside, and prior sources of support may be described as untrustworthy, ignorant, or hostile. This exclusivity matters because it removes corrective input. Without meaningful contact with people who can offer alternative interpretations, the shared belief is less likely to be challenged and more likely to harden. Case reports of shared delusional states repeatedly describe this kind of isolation or near-isolation as part of the relational setting in which the condition develops [1][9][4].

Another escalating pattern is reassurance seeking that never resolves. At first, one person may ask for confirmation, and the other may provide it to reduce anxiety. Over time, however, reassurance becomes a ritual that feeds the belief rather than calms it. The pair may repeatedly review the same "evidence," revisit the same suspicions, or search for new signs that support the shared interpretation. Each cycle gives the impression of careful reasoning, yet the structure of the conversation is circular. Doubt is not examined; it is managed as a threat. This is especially concerning when the relationship rewards intensity over reflection, because the more emotional the exchange becomes, the more convincing the belief may feel.

Escalating risk is also signaled by increasing dominance in interpretation. One person may begin to set the terms of what is real, what is important, and what must be done. The other person may defer out of fear, admiration, gratitude, or habit. This is not always obvious coercion. Sometimes it takes the form of subtle correction: "You're misunderstanding," "You're too sensitive," or "Don't tell anyone; they won't get it." Over time, the relationship can develop an internal hierarchy in which one person's certainty functions like a rule and the other person's uncertainty is treated as weakness. When that hierarchy is present, the secondary person may adopt the belief not only because it seems plausible, but because disagreement has become relationally costly.

A further red flag is progressive withdrawal from shared reality with others. The pair may stop discussing concerns with family, avoid medical or mental health consultation, or reinterpret outside feedback as proof of persecution or misunderstanding. In some cases, they become increasingly private about daily routines, communications, or whereabouts. Privacy alone is not pathological, but in the context of a developing shared delusion, secrecy often serves to protect the belief from scrutiny. A relationship that once tolerated outside input now treats it as intrusion. That shift matters because clinical deterioration often advances fastest when the dyad becomes self-referential and no longer checks its assumptions against broader social reality.

Risk also rises when the relationship shows mutual amplification of fear. One person expresses suspicion, and the other adds detail; one person becomes alarmed, and the other escalates the interpretation from concern to certainty. The emotional tone itself becomes evidence. This can be seen in pairs who repeatedly reinforce each other's vigilance, anger, or dread until ordinary events are recast as confirmation. In some presentations, the belief content is less important than the emotional pattern around it: hypervigilance, urgency, and a shared sense that immediate action is required. When fear is continuously validated, it can become the organizing principle of the relationship, leaving little room for doubt or recovery.

Clinicians and caregivers should pay particular attention when these patterns begin to affect functioning, safety, and autonomy. Escalation is suggested when daily life is increasingly arranged around the belief, when one person's choices are narrowing the other's options, or when the pair shows growing hostility toward anyone who questions them. The relationship may become more rigid, more secretive, and more difficult to interrupt. In that setting, the issue is no longer simply that two people share an unusual idea. The concern is that the relationship itself is becoming the mechanism that sustains the delusion, protects it from reality testing, and deepens its hold on both people [6][2][3].

When unusual beliefs become clinically concerning

Unusual beliefs become clinically concerning when they stop functioning as isolated ideas and begin to organize perception, emotion, and behavior. At that point, the question is no longer whether a person has an eccentric opinion or a private interpretation, but whether the belief is becoming resistant to ordinary correction and increasingly costly to daily life. A belief that once seemed merely odd can take on clinical significance when it becomes fixed, self-sealing, and increasingly disconnected from shared evidence. In shared psychotic disorder, this process often unfolds within a relationship, so the concern is not only the content of the belief but the way it is being maintained between two people.

One important marker is the degree of conviction. People can hold strong opinions without being delusional, but clinical concern rises when the person cannot realistically entertain alternative explanations, even briefly. If every contradiction is reinterpreted as proof, if every absence of evidence is treated as concealment, or if reassurance only deepens the belief, the pattern suggests that reality testing is narrowing. The belief may still sound organized and logical on the surface, which is part of what makes these cases difficult to recognize. The problem is not disorganization alone; it is the closed circuit in which the idea continually protects itself from revision.

Another warning sign is behavioral escalation. A belief becomes more concerning when it begins to drive monitoring, avoidance, confrontation, secrecy, or repeated attempts to "verify" what is happening. The person may change routines, limit contact with outsiders, or reorganize the household around the suspected threat. Sleep, appetite, work, and social engagement may begin to suffer because so much attention is being pulled toward the belief. In a shared presentation, both individuals may adapt their behavior in ways that reinforce the same interpretation, making the belief feel more credible simply because the relationship has been reshaped around it.

Clinically, it is also important to look for loss of proportionality. Many people experience fears, suspicions, or unusual interpretations during stress, grief, or conflict. Those experiences become more concerning when the emotional response is far greater than the available evidence would justify and when the response remains intense despite repeated reassurance. A person may insist that a neighbor, relative, employer, or stranger is part of a coordinated plot, even though no concrete proof exists. If the belief leads to persistent distress, impaired functioning, or escalating interpersonal conflict, it is no longer just a strange idea; it is a clinically relevant impairment in judgment and reality testing.

The relational context matters just as much. In shared psychotic disorder, the secondary person often appears less certain at first, but concern increases when that person begins to mirror the primary person's conviction, language, and emotional intensity. The secondary person may initially express hesitation, then gradually adopt the same explanations, the same suspicions, and the same defensive posture toward outsiders. In rare but documented cases, more than two people can be drawn into the same delusional framework, underscoring how strongly a closed relational system can sustain shared belief [12]. When multiple people reinforce one another without meaningful outside feedback, the belief can become harder to challenge and easier to normalize.

It is equally important to distinguish concern from mere difference. People may hold unconventional religious, political, or cultural beliefs without being psychotic, and mental health professionals must avoid pathologizing beliefs simply because they are unfamiliar. The clinical question is whether the belief is idiosyncratic, fixed beyond evidence, and causing impairment or danger. A belief becomes especially concerning when it is paired with suspiciousness, fear-based decision-making, or actions that could place the person or others at risk. The more the belief governs choices, narrows relationships, and resists any testing against reality, the more it deserves careful assessment rather than casual dismissal.

Finally, unusual beliefs are clinically concerning when they begin to outgrow the context that first gave them shape. A fear that starts as a response to a real stressor may become detached from the original event, expanding into a broader system of explanations that absorbs everything around it. At that stage, the belief is no longer simply a reaction; it has become an organizing framework. In shared psychotic disorder, that framework is often sustained by closeness, dependency, and repeated mutual confirmation. The more the relationship itself becomes the main source of "evidence," the more urgent it is to assess whether the belief is crossing from private meaning into psychopathology.

CHAPTER 4

Chapter 4: Causes, Risk Factors, and Vulnerabilities

Understanding why shared psychotic disorder takes hold requires looking at the conditions that make a delusion easier to absorb, harder to question, and more likely to persist inside a close relationship. The pattern rarely rests on one cause alone. Instead, susceptibility tends to emerge where personal history, emotional strain, relational structure, and limited outside reality-testing converge. In some cases, an already fragile sense of stability leaves a person more open to adopting another's certainty; in others, the surrounding environment gradually narrows the range of perspectives available. Clinical reports repeatedly show that the disorder is most likely to develop in settings where closeness is intense and external correction is weak [1][9][4].

Preexisting psychiatric conditions and susceptibility

Preexisting psychiatric conditions can shape both the form and the direction of susceptibility. A person does not need a prior diagnosis for shared psychotic disorder to emerge, but certain vulnerabilities can make it easier for another person's beliefs to take hold. These vulnerabilities are often less about a single disorder than about a broader weakening of reality testing, emotional regulation, or interpersonal independence. When someone already struggles with anxiety, depression, obsessive thinking, personality pathology, or a history of psychotic symptoms, the mind may be more likely to search for certainty, cling to explanations that reduce distress, or defer too readily to a dominant relationship figure.

One important distinction is that a preexisting condition does not automatically produce shared delusion. It creates a context in which influence can become more powerful. For example, a person with chronic anxiety may be highly sensitive to threat and therefore more likely to interpret ambiguous events as confirming danger. Someone with obsessive-compulsive traits may become locked into repetitive doubt and reassurance-seeking, which can make a partner's fixed belief feel like relief rather than distortion. A person with borderline personality features may experience abandonment fears so intensely that disagreement feels intolerable, leading them to preserve attachment by adopting the other person's view. In each case, the preexisting condition changes how the person weighs evidence, tolerates uncertainty, and manages interpersonal pressure.

Psychotic disorders and psychosis-spectrum histories are especially relevant because they can blur the boundary between an induced belief and an independently generated one. If a person has experienced hallucinations, delusional thinking, or episodes of impaired reality testing in the past, it may be clinically difficult to determine whether a shared belief is truly secondary, partially autonomous, or simply co-occurring alongside another illness. This is one reason careful assessment matters: what appears to be "shared" may actually reflect a vulnerable person whose own psychiatric illness is being shaped, amplified, or organized by the relationship. Case literature has described unusual multi-person presentations, including folie à trois, where a delusional idea spreads through a family system and is reinforced by existing medical and psychiatric fragility [12].

Depression can also increase susceptibility, particularly when it is severe enough to narrow perspective and reduce confidence in one's own judgment. A depressed person may become passive, dependent, or desperate for explanation, especially if life circumstances already feel unmanageable. In that state, a partner's or caregiver's certainty can seem stabilizing. Trauma-related conditions may contribute in a similar way. People with histories of abuse, coercion, or chronic invalidation may have learned to distrust their own perceptions or to survive by aligning quickly with a powerful other. That learned adaptation can become a liability when the other person's beliefs are distorted. What once served as protection can become a pathway to adoption of the shared delusion.

Personality structure matters as well, though it should not be treated as destiny. Individuals with dependent traits may be especially vulnerable because they rely heavily on another person for direction, emotional regulation, and reality confirmation. Those with avoidant traits may be less likely to seek outside feedback once a relationship becomes their main source of safety. Paranoid traits can increase the likelihood that suspicious ideas will feel plausible, while schizotypal traits may make unusual interpretations feel less foreign. The clinical point is not to reduce susceptibility to a label, but to recognize how enduring patterns of relating and thinking can create openings for distorted shared beliefs to settle in.

Medication status, cognitive impairment, and substance use can further complicate the picture. A person who is intoxicated, withdrawing, sleep-deprived, or cognitively slowed may have less capacity to challenge implausible claims. Likewise, someone with neurodevelopmental differences or acquired brain injury may be more dependent on routine, authority, or a familiar interpersonal system, which can increase the influence of a dominant partner or family member. These factors do not cause shared psychotic disorder on their own, but they can lower the threshold at which a delusional framework begins to feel coherent and emotionally necessary.

For clinicians, the practical question is not simply whether a patient has a diagnosis, but how that diagnosis affects dependence, suggestibility, and access to alternative reality checks. A preexisting psychiatric condition becomes especially relevant when it reduces autonomy, intensifies fear, or makes disagreement feel unsafe. The more a person's symptoms push them toward isolation, reassurance-seeking, or reliance on one powerful relationship, the easier it becomes for a shared belief to take root and persist. In that sense, susceptibility is often the product of an illness interacting with a relationship, not of either one alone.

Trauma, chronic stress, and adverse life experiences

Trauma can shape shared psychotic disorder long before any delusional belief becomes visible. When a person has lived through abuse, neglect, betrayal, domestic violence, or repeated instability, the mind may become organized around vigilance rather than flexibility. That state does not produce a shared delusion by itself, but it can make unusual explanations feel emotionally necessary. A frightening interpretation may seem preferable to uncertainty because it gives suffering a name, a cause, and a target. In that sense, trauma can narrow the range of meanings a person can tolerate. When another individual enters that narrowed field with certainty, the belief may land with unusual force.

Chronic stress works in a similar way, but through accumulation rather than a single event. A person who is constantly overwhelmed often has less access to reflective thinking, less patience for ambiguity, and less ability to compare impressions against outside evidence. Sleep disruption, hyperarousal, and persistent fear can weaken judgment and increase reliance on immediate emotional cues. Under those conditions, a partner, parent, sibling, or caregiver who speaks with confidence may become the most available source of reality. If that source repeatedly frames ordinary events as threatening, the stressed person may gradually adopt the same interpretation simply because it feels more coherent than the chaos they are already living in.

Adverse life experiences also matter because they can create a deep expectation that danger is hidden and that other people cannot be trusted. This expectation may not appear as a delusion at first. It can begin as guardedness, suspiciousness, or a sense that the world is unsafe. But when such expectations are reinforced inside an intense relationship, they may harden into a shared narrative. A person who has learned that their own perceptions were ignored or invalidated may be especially vulnerable to accepting someone else's account over their own. The result is not merely agreement; it is a kind of psychological surrender, in which external certainty replaces internal doubt.

For the secondary person, trauma history can be especially important when it is paired with dependency. Someone who has been emotionally injured may cling tightly to a relationship that offers protection, identity, or belonging. If the more dominant person also carries a delusional framework, the secondary person may absorb it as part of the cost of staying connected. The belief can become entangled with loyalty: to question the idea feels like risking abandonment, conflict, or further harm. This is one reason shared psychotic disorder is often seen in relationships where one person's emotional security depends heavily on the other's approval or guidance [1][9][2].

In clinical practice, trauma can also blur the line between realistic caution and distorted conviction. A person who has been genuinely harmed may have good reason to be wary, which makes it harder to distinguish protective alertness from an emerging delusional system. That ambiguity can delay recognition. The beliefs may be partly grounded in real events, then extended beyond them in ways that are no longer proportionate. For example, a real conflict, a past intrusion, or a legitimate medical complaint may become the starting point for a much broader narrative of persecution, contamination, surveillance, or betrayal. Once the narrative begins to organize every new experience, the relationship itself can become the main engine of persistence.

Adverse experiences in childhood are particularly relevant because they can shape attachment, self-trust, and tolerance for uncertainty for years afterward. A person raised in an environment of fear or inconsistency may become highly attuned to emotional cues and highly reliant on the judgment of others. That pattern can make them more responsive to a strong personality who offers certainty, even when the certainty is false. It can also make separation feel intolerable, which is why some shared delusions remain in place until the relationship changes or outside support becomes unavoidable. Case reports continue to show that these dynamics are often embedded in close, isolated bonds rather than occurring in a social vacuum [6][8][4].

None of this means that trauma causes shared psychotic disorder in a simple or direct way. Many people with significant trauma histories never develop psychosis, and many people with shared delusions have no obvious trauma exposure. What trauma, chronic stress, and adverse life experiences do is increase vulnerability by weakening the person's confidence in their own perceptions and by making external certainty feel emotionally safer than independent judgment. In that setting, the shared belief is not only a symptom to be observed; it is often a strategy the mind uses to survive fear, disconnection, and prolonged distress.

Social isolation, dependency, and limited external feedback

Social isolation does more than reduce contact with other people; it narrows the field in which beliefs can be tested. When a relationship becomes the main, or only, source of emotional contact, the people inside it lose access to the small but important corrections that ordinarily come from ordinary conversation. A neighbor's puzzled look, a friend's practical question, a coworker's different interpretation, or a relative's calm disagreement can interrupt a distorted idea before it hardens. Without those interruptions, a shared belief is more likely to circulate unchallenged and begin to feel self-evident. In that sense, isolation is not merely a background condition. It is part of the mechanism that allows the delusional framework to become internally convincing.

This narrowing often develops gradually. The pair may withdraw for reasons that seem understandable at first: conflict with family, distrust of outsiders, financial strain, illness, caregiving demands, relocation, or a sense that no one else "understands" the relationship. Over time, each reason for staying inside the dyad can become a reason to stay there even more. The more time the two people spend together, the more their conversations become repetitive, and the more their shared interpretation of events is reinforced by itself. Even ordinary ambiguities—an unanswered phone call, a comment from a stranger, a delayed appointment—can be absorbed into the same explanatory system because there are fewer competing viewpoints available to challenge it.

Dependency deepens this process by making disagreement feel costly. When one person relies on the other for housing, money, transportation, emotional regulation, decision-making, or a sense of identity, the relationship is no longer just intimate; it becomes structurally difficult to question. The dependent person may learn that preserving closeness matters more than examining whether the belief is accurate. In some cases, the dependent person does not consciously "choose" the belief so much as accommodate it in order to maintain stability, avoid abandonment, or reduce conflict. The result is not simple agreement but a form of psychological adaptation in which reality testing is subordinated to attachment needs.

Limited external feedback is what allows that adaptation to persist. Most people live inside a web of low-stakes reality checks: casual disagreement, shared routines, institutional boundaries, and practical consequences. These forms of feedback are easy to overlook when they are present, but they are essential to keeping unusual ideas from becoming fixed. When they are absent, the relationship can develop its own closed logic. Statements are not examined for accuracy so much as for whether they fit the emotional atmosphere of the dyad. Doubt is reinterpreted as disloyalty, and outside input is treated as ignorance, hostility, or evidence of the very threat the pair already fears. In clinical descriptions of shared psychosis, this isolation from broader social contact is a recurring theme [9][4].

The danger is not only that the belief goes unchallenged, but that the relationship begins to supply its own proof. Two people who spend nearly all their time together may notice the same events, repeat the same interpretations, and gradually lose the ability to separate observation from explanation. A vague concern can be revisited so often that it acquires the weight of fact. A frightened reaction from one person can become confirmation for the other. In families or caregiving settings, where roles already include dependence and authority, the absence of outside perspective can be especially powerful because the same person may control both the interpretation of events and the response to them.

It is important to distinguish isolation from simple privacy. Many close relationships are private without being pathological. The clinical concern arises when privacy becomes exclusionary, when the pair's world becomes so closed that no one else can meaningfully influence what they believe or how they behave. At that point, the relationship is no longer just a site where a delusion is shared; it is the environment that protects the delusion from correction. That protection can be reinforced by shame, fear of stigma, or a history of being dismissed by others, all of which make outside contact feel risky. For clinicians and caregivers, the practical significance of this pattern is that the social environment itself may need to be addressed, not only the belief content.

Seen this way, social isolation, dependency, and limited external feedback are not separate risks but interlocking conditions. Isolation reduces corrective input, dependency raises the emotional cost of disagreement, and the lack of outside feedback allows the shared interpretation to become a closed system. Together, they create a setting in which an unusual belief can feel increasingly reasonable simply because nothing remains in the person's life to test it against. That is why assessing shared psychotic disorder requires attention not only to what the person believes, but also to who is available to question it, who has the power to define it, and what would happen if the relationship were exposed to a broader reality.

Family systems, caregiving contexts, and high-control relationships

Family systems can create a particularly durable setting for shared psychotic disorder because they organize not only daily routines but also the emotional rules of belonging. In some households, the family is so tightly structured around one person's fears, interpretations, or demands that disagreement becomes difficult to express without consequences. Over time, the family may adapt to the delusional framework in practical ways: conversations narrow, outside relationships weaken, and decisions are made to reduce conflict rather than to test reality. What begins as an effort to keep peace can gradually become a pattern of accommodation that protects the belief from challenge. In that sense, the family system does not merely surround the delusion; it can help stabilize it.

This is especially true when roles are rigid and emotionally loaded. A parent may be treated as the unquestioned authority, a dependent adult child may be cast as the loyal protector, or a spouse may become the constant interpreter of danger. Once those roles harden, family members can feel that questioning the shared belief is equivalent to betraying the relationship itself. The result is often a closed loop in which fear is repeatedly confirmed by the very people who are trying to reduce distress. Clinical reports have described shared delusional patterns arising in family settings, including parent-child dynamics and multi-person household arrangements [8][9]. These cases do not imply that families cause psychosis in a simple linear way; rather, they show how family structure can make a false belief more difficult to dislodge once it has taken hold.

Caregiving contexts add another layer of complexity because caregiving is built on trust, dependence, and the assumption that one person can reliably interpret another's needs. When the caregiver is also the source of the unusual belief, the recipient may have very little room to compare perspectives or seek correction. This is particularly important when the person receiving care is elderly, medically vulnerable, cognitively impaired, or socially isolated. A caregiver's certainty can be mistaken for expertise, especially if the dependent person already feels frightened, confused, or ashamed. In such situations, the delusional belief may be woven into ordinary acts of assistance—medication schedules, hygiene routines, monitoring of symptoms, or explanations for bodily discomfort—until the belief becomes part of the caregiving script itself.

The reverse can also occur: a caregiver may begin by trying to manage another person's distress and gradually become absorbed into the same explanatory system. Repeated exposure to the same alarming story, especially without outside feedback, can shift the caregiver from skeptical observer to active participant. This is one reason shared psychotic disorder can persist in settings where the caregiving role is intense and socially isolated. The caregiver may feel responsible for preventing catastrophe, while the dependent person feels safer when the caregiver appears to confirm the threat. Each person's behavior then strengthens the other's conviction. In clinical practice, this pattern can be difficult to separate from ordinary caregiver stress unless the relational dynamics are examined directly.

High-control relationships are another common context in which shared beliefs become entrenched. These relationships are not defined only by overt intimidation; they may also involve emotional manipulation, surveillance, isolation, or the steady erosion of independent judgment. The dominant person may control access to information, frame all disagreement as disloyalty, and present their own interpretations as the only trustworthy account of events. Over time, the less powerful person may stop consulting their own impressions because doing so feels dangerous or futile. In that environment, a delusional belief can function as part of a broader system of control, not merely as a symptom occurring alongside it. The belief may justify restrictions, explain away external concern, or deepen dependence by making the outside world seem threatening.

It is important, however, not to overgeneralize. Not every intense relationship is pathological, and not every family that becomes preoccupied with a disturbing idea is experiencing shared psychotic disorder. Some families are responding to genuine danger, medical uncertainty, domestic violence, or a history of betrayal that has made mistrust understandable. The clinical task is to ask whether the belief is resistant to evidence, whether it is narrowing the person's access to reality, and whether the relationship is amplifying that narrowing through repetition, fear, or coercion. The presence of conflict, protectiveness, or unusual closeness alone is not enough. What matters is whether the relationship is becoming the main engine that keeps a fixed false belief alive [1][4].

For that reason, assessment in these settings must look beyond the content of the belief and into the structure of dependence around it. Who has the power to define what is happening? Who is isolated from outside contact? Who is expected to comply, reassure, or remain silent? Who benefits from the belief, and who is constrained by it? These questions are not meant to assign blame, but to clarify the relational conditions that allow shared delusions to persist. In family systems, caregiving arrangements, and high-control relationships, the symptom is often inseparable from the interpersonal environment that sustains it. Recognizing that environment is often the first step in understanding why the belief has become so resistant to change.

CHAPTER 5

Chapter 5: Assessment and Differential Diagnosis

Assessment in shared psychotic disorder begins with a careful effort to understand not only what each person believes, but how those beliefs are organized, sustained, and affected by the relationship itself. Because the presentation can resemble other psychotic, mood-related, medical, or relational conditions, the clinician has to move deliberately and avoid assuming that the shared quality of the belief tells the whole story. The task is not simply to identify an unusual idea, but to determine whether it reflects a broader syndrome, a secondary response to another person's psychopathology, or something else entirely.

Clinical interview strategies and history-taking priorities

Clinical interviewing in suspected shared psychotic disorder has to be organized around two simultaneous questions: what each person believes, and how the relationship has shaped the belief's persistence. The interviewer is not simply collecting symptoms in parallel; the task is to reconstruct a relational sequence. That means paying close attention to who first described the unusual idea, how the second person responded, and whether the belief has been strengthened by closeness, repetition, fear, or isolation. Because the syndrome is uncommon and still somewhat elusive in the literature [1], the history often matters more than the label at the first encounter.

The first priority is to separate the content of the belief from the process by which it is maintained. A careful interviewer asks open, nonconfrontational questions that allow each person to describe events in their own words before any comparison is made. It is often useful to ask when the concern began, what changed in the relationship around that time, and whether the belief grew gradually or appeared suddenly after contact with a more convinced person. The goal is not to challenge the belief too early, but to understand its internal logic, its emotional function, and the degree to which it has become embedded in daily routines. In cases reported in the literature, the shared belief may appear in close family or partner relationships and can be reinforced by isolation from broader social feedback [9][2].

Equally important is identifying the role of each participant. The more dominant or more symptomatic person may not always be the one who speaks most forcefully in the interview, and the less vocal person may still be the one whose conviction is most fixed. Interviewers should avoid assuming that the first person to speak is the primary case or that the more passive person is merely "going along." Instead, it helps to ask each person separately about their own certainty, doubts, and willingness to consider alternative explanations. A useful line of inquiry is whether either person has ever questioned the belief privately but felt unable to express that doubt in the relationship. That question often reveals the degree of dependency, fear of conflict, or emotional coercion that keeps the shared system intact.

History-taking should also focus on the broader context that makes shared belief more likely to flourish. Social isolation, caregiving dependence, chronic stress, and limited contact with outside perspectives can all narrow reality-testing and make the relationship itself the main source of validation. The interviewer should ask about living arrangements, daily routines, access to friends or relatives, recent losses, and any changes in work, housing, or health that may have intensified closeness. When the relationship is highly enclosed, even ordinary conversations can become part of the delusional reinforcement loop. In some cases, the belief is not simply "shared" in a psychological sense; it is sustained through a practical system in which one person's interpretation becomes the other's only available framework.

Another priority is to establish the timeline of symptom emergence and look for evidence of an underlying psychotic or mood disorder in either person. Shared psychotic disorder is not diagnosed by the presence of a strange belief alone; the clinician must consider whether one person has an independent primary psychotic illness, a mood disorder with psychotic features, substance-related symptoms, or a medical condition that better explains the presentation. This is especially important because the shared belief may obscure a more conventional psychiatric picture. Careful questioning about hallucinations, disorganization, sleep disruption, mania, depression, trauma history, substance use, and medication adherence can help determine whether the delusion is truly induced or whether both individuals are expressing symptoms of another disorder. Case reports of shared delusional infestation, for example, often emphasize the need to rule out medical causes before concluding that the belief is psychotic in origin [5][7].

Collateral information is often indispensable, but it must be gathered with discretion. Family members, primary care clinicians, therapists, emergency responders, and even prior records may provide details that the couple or family cannot describe coherently in session. The interviewer should compare accounts for consistency without turning the encounter into an adversarial fact-checking exercise. Discrepancies are clinically useful when they show how the belief is organized, but the process should remain focused on safety, function, and pattern rather than on proving anyone wrong. In some presentations, the unusual belief has spread to more than two people, which makes it especially important to ask who else in the environment has adopted, resisted, or quietly accommodated the idea [8].

Finally, the interview should assess insight, risk, and immediate containment needs from the beginning. A person may be calm while describing a fixed delusion and still be at risk if the belief has begun to drive self-harm, violence, refusal of care, or escalating confrontation with outsiders. Questions about fear, intent, defensive behavior, and recent actions are essential, especially when the pair appears highly fused or emotionally dependent. The clinician should also note whether either person can tolerate any uncertainty at all. Even a small capacity to say, "I am not completely sure," can be clinically meaningful, because it suggests that the belief has not become entirely impermeable. In shared psychotic disorder, that sliver of doubt may be one of the most important findings in the entire history.

Using collateral sources and observing relational patterns

Collateral information is often what separates a vague suspicion from a clinically usable picture. In shared psychotic disorder, each person's account may be shaped by loyalty, fear, shame, confusion, or an effort to protect the relationship. That means the interview data gathered from the pair alone can be incomplete in ways that matter. Family members, roommates, prior clinicians, primary care providers, school personnel, employers, and in some cases neighbors or case managers may supply details about the onset of the belief, the sequence of events, and the degree to which the two people have become isolated from outside feedback. The goal is not to build a case against anyone; it is to reconstruct how the belief entered the relationship, how it has been maintained, and what changed in functioning when the shared conviction intensified.

Collateral sources are especially useful for establishing chronology. A delusional belief that appears to be "shared" may actually have begun as a concern voiced by one person and then adopted by the other after weeks or months of repetitive discussion. In other situations, the second person may have had doubts at first but gradually stopped voicing them because disagreement led to conflict, withdrawal, or emotional punishment. These distinctions matter because they help the clinician identify the likely primary and secondary roles, while also recognizing that those roles are not always fixed. A person who seems secondary in one setting may appear more dominant in another, and the balance can shift over time as illness severity, dependency, or stress changes. Reports from people outside the dyad can reveal whether the belief was already present in one person before the relationship became more closed and reinforcing.

Observing relational patterns in real time can be just as informative as the history itself. The way the two people speak to each other during an interview often shows whether the relationship is organized around correction, protection, submission, or shared alarm. One person may answer for the other, finish sentences, or subtly police what can be said. The other may glance for approval before responding, defer quickly, or appear to monitor the emotional temperature of the room. Clinicians should pay attention not only to the content of statements but to the process by which statements are made, revised, or withdrawn. A shared delusion often lives inside a pattern of mutual reinforcement: one person introduces or intensifies the idea, and the other responds with deference, urgency, or selective agreement, which then strengthens the first person's confidence.

It is also important to notice how the pair reacts when the conversation moves toward ordinary reality testing. Does one person become visibly anxious when the other expresses doubt? Does the more dominant member interrupt, correct, or dismiss outside perspectives before they can be considered? Do both individuals quickly shift into a rehearsed explanation that leaves no room for ambiguity? These reactions can be more telling than the delusional claim itself. In many cases, the shared belief is protected by a relational rule: uncertainty is treated as disloyalty, and outside disagreement is reframed as ignorance, hostility, or evidence of the delusion's truth. That rule can be visible in tone, posture, timing, and the speed with which the pair returns to a mutually defended interpretation.

Collateral observation can also clarify the extent of social narrowing. A close pair may describe themselves as simply private or mutually supportive, while outside contacts report a more concerning pattern: the two rarely separate, no longer maintain prior friendships, avoid family gatherings, or interpret ordinary questions as threats.

Sometimes the relationship has become the main source of meaning, reassurance, and decision-making, which leaves little room for corrective input. Case reports have shown that shared delusional systems can develop not only in face-to-face isolation but also through sustained remote contact, including telephone-based interaction [3], reminding clinicians that relational reinforcement does not require constant physical proximity. What matters is the repeated exchange through which the belief is sustained and insulated from challenge.

Because shared psychotic disorder can overlap with other psychotic, mood-related, or trauma-related conditions, collateral sources should not be used simply to confirm a favorite diagnosis. They are most valuable when they help the clinician compare perspectives and identify inconsistencies that point toward a broader differential. A medical record may show prior psychotic symptoms in one person, a history of substance use, or a recent stressor that changed the relationship's stability. Another informant may describe one person as increasingly fearful, controlling, or withdrawn long before the second person adopted the same belief. In family settings, especially where roles are entrenched, the pattern may resemble a system in which one person's certainty becomes the household's organizing principle [9]. That kind of information can be crucial for deciding whether the shared belief is best understood as a primary psychotic process, a relationally maintained delusion, or part of a more complex clinical picture [1][2][4].

Careful observation also helps the clinician avoid being pulled into the dyad's preferred narrative. A pair may present with polished coherence, especially if they have rehearsed the story repeatedly or learned that outside professionals are to be managed rather than engaged. The clinician's task is to remain attentive to emotional alignment, shifts in dominance, and the degree to which each person can think independently when separated. When possible, brief individual interviews can be revealing, not because they automatically expose the truth, but because they show whether the belief loosens when the relational pressure is reduced. In shared psychotic disorder, the relationship itself is part of the symptom picture, so the way the two people relate to each other is not ancillary data. It is often one of the most important sources of evidence available.

Differential diagnosis: what to rule out and why

Effective differential diagnosis in shared psychotic disorder begins with restraint. The clinician has to resist the temptation to name the relational pattern too quickly, because the shared quality of a belief can appear in several different conditions, and some of them require very different interventions. What matters first is whether the unusual belief is best explained by a primary psychotic disorder in one or both people, a mood disorder with psychotic features, a medical or neurologic condition, substance use, or a nonpsychotic relational process that only resembles delusion from the outside. The label should follow the pattern, not replace the work of understanding it.

One of the most important conditions to rule out is schizophrenia spectrum illness in the person who appears to be the source of the belief. Shared psychotic disorder can sometimes mask a more established psychotic disorder, especially when the more impaired person is also the more persuasive one. If hallucinations, disorganized speech, marked negative symptoms, bizarre behavior, or a long-standing decline in functioning are present, the clinician should consider whether the case is better understood as schizophrenia, schizophreniform disorder, or another primary psychotic illness rather than a separately transmitted delusional system. The distinction matters because the apparent "shared" belief may simply be one expression of a broader psychotic process in the first person, with the second person responding to that illness in a dependent or suggestible way.

Mood disorders with psychotic features also need careful exclusion. A person whose belief intensifies only during a major depressive episode or a manic episode may not fit the pattern of shared psychosis at all. In major depression, guilt, nihilism, poverty, or deserved punishment can become delusional in a way that is tightly bound to the mood state. In mania, grandiosity, special mission themes, and expansive certainty may dominate the clinical picture. If the delusion appears only during mood episodes, or if mood symptoms clearly precede and organize the psychosis, the diagnosis shifts away from shared psychotic disorder. This distinction is especially important because treating the mood disorder may reduce the psychotic content without needing to conceptualize the belief as socially transmitted.

Substance-induced psychosis and medical causes must also be ruled out before the relational explanation is accepted. Stimulants, cannabis, alcohol withdrawal, hallucinogens, corticosteroids, and other medications can all produce paranoia, unusual conviction, or perceptual disturbance. Likewise, neurologic illness, endocrine disturbance, autoimmune conditions, infections, sleep deprivation, and delirium can present with confusion or fixed false beliefs that may be mistaken for delusion. A shared presentation can mislead the clinician into focusing on the relationship while missing a biological driver in one or both individuals. When symptoms are acute, fluctuating, associated with cognitive change, or accompanied by abnormal physical findings, the threshold for medical evaluation should be low. Case reports of delusional infestation, for example, repeatedly show the need to exclude medical explanations before concluding that the belief is psychotic in origin [5][7].

It is also necessary to distinguish shared psychotic disorder from overvalued ideas, culturally shared beliefs, and intense but nonpsychotic family systems. Some groups hold unusual beliefs that are not delusional because they remain open to discussion, are embedded in a broader cultural or religious context, and do not produce the kind of rigid, self-sealing certainty typical of psychosis. Even in highly enmeshed relationships, two people may reinforce each other's fears without crossing into delusion. The clinician has to ask whether the belief is truly fixed despite contrary evidence, whether it is idiosyncratic rather than culturally sanctioned, and whether it has begun to impair judgment or functioning. Without that distinction, there is a risk of pathologizing grief, suspicion, superstition, or family conflict as if it were psychosis.

Paranoid personality traits, obsessive preoccupation, and trauma-related hypervigilance can also resemble shared psychosis from a distance. A person who is chronically mistrustful may interpret ordinary events as threatening without losing contact with reality in the broader sense. Someone with obsessive concerns may repeatedly seek reassurance, gather evidence, and remain distressed by intrusive doubts, yet still recognize that the fear may be irrational. Trauma survivors may scan for danger and develop rigid explanations as a way of managing fear. These presentations can look delusional if the clinician focuses only on the content of the belief rather than on the person's capacity for reflection, doubt, and revision. Shared psychotic disorder becomes more likely when conviction is imported through a relationship and then maintained by mutual reinforcement, rather than emerging from a stable personality style or anxiety pattern alone.

The relationship itself can help clarify the diagnosis, but it should not be treated as proof by itself. In shared psychotic disorder, the more convincing figure is often the person with greater dominance, greater psychological organization, or a more established psychotic process, while the second person's belief tends to soften when separated from that influence [1][6][9][4]. If the second person's symptoms quickly diminish after distance, that supports the possibility of a shared syndrome, but it does not end the diagnostic work. The clinician still has to determine whether the second person had an independent psychotic disorder that was merely obscured by the relationship, or whether separation simply reduced exposure to a reinforcing environment. Several recent case reports continue to describe the importance of relational context, including family and remote contact patterns, in understanding how shared delusions develop and persist [8][3].

For that reason, the differential diagnosis is not a one-time sorting exercise but a sequence of eliminations and refinements. The question is not only "What belief is being shared?" but "What else could account for this presentation, and what evidence would make that explanation more likely?" When the answer points toward primary psychosis, mood disorder, substance use, medical illness, cultural context, or a nonpsychotic relational pattern, the label of shared psychotic disorder should be used cautiously or not at all. When those possibilities are reasonably excluded and the delusional content is clearly sustained through close relational contact, the diagnosis becomes more clinically meaningful and the treatment plan more precise.

Assessing risk, insight, and immediate safety concerns

Assessment begins with a practical question: how dangerous is the situation right now, and who is at immediate risk if the shared belief continues to govern behavior? In shared psychotic disorder, risk is not limited to the content of the delusion itself. It also arises from what the belief is prompting the people involved to do, avoid, or tolerate. A conviction about being watched, poisoned, infested, targeted, or spiritually attacked may lead to confrontation, self-injury, medical refusal, repeated checking, fleeing, retaliatory behavior, or escalating dependence on the person who appears to "know what is true." The clinician has to look beyond the belief and evaluate the behavioral consequences already unfolding.

Immediate safety concerns often become visible through urgency, agitation, or a sudden change in functioning. A person may be sleeping poorly, eating less, avoiding normal activities, or becoming increasingly preoccupied with protective routines. In some cases, the distress is expressed as panic, hopelessness, or suicidal thinking, especially when the person feels trapped inside the belief or unable to escape the relationship organizing it. Case reports of shared delusional states have included emergency presentations with suicidal ideation or severe distress related to the delusional experience [7]. When that level of distress is present, the assessment must move quickly toward stabilization rather than prolonged exploration of the belief's logic.

Risk assessment also needs to distinguish between the primary and secondary person without assuming that only one of them is vulnerable. The person who appears to be the originator of the belief may be more likely to show agitation, hostility, or rigid conviction, but the person who has adopted the belief can be equally at risk if they are dependent, fearful, or cut off from outside support. In family-based or highly isolated presentations, the relationship may function as a closed system in which both people reinforce one another's alarm and both become less able to reality-test against the wider environment [9]. In those settings, the question is not simply who "has" the delusion, but whether either person can still pause, reflect, and accept help.

Insight is central because it shapes whether the person can collaborate with care. Insight in this context does not mean full agreement with the clinician; it means some capacity to consider that the belief may be mistaken, exaggerated, or influenced by the relationship. A person with partial insight may still be frightened or uncertain, but they can usually describe doubt, ambivalence, or moments when the evidence did not fit. By contrast, absent insight is marked by certainty, defensiveness, and a tendency to reinterpret every contradiction as proof of the belief. Shared psychotic disorder can be especially difficult to assess because the secondary person may appear more open at first while still remaining deeply committed to the shared framework once the relationship is activated.

It is also important to assess whether insight is being actively suppressed by interpersonal pressure. A clinician may encounter a person who privately acknowledges uncertainty but quickly retracts it in the presence of the dominant partner, parent, or caregiver. That pattern suggests not only psychological dependence but possible coercion, intimidation, or fear of abandonment. In such cases, the apparent absence of insight may be partly relational rather than purely cognitive. The interview should therefore include attention to who answers for whom, who interrupts, who dismisses doubt, and whether the person can speak differently when separated from the other member of the pair. Shared delusions documented in close relationships, including family settings and even prolonged contact at a distance, show how strongly the relational channel can shape conviction [8][3][4].

Immediate safety concerns should also include the possibility of medical harm. Shared beliefs sometimes lead to unnecessary treatments, refusal of appropriate care, overuse of cleaning or disinfecting products, skin damage from scratching or picking, or unsafe attempts to remove an imagined source of danger. When the belief centers on infestation, contamination, poisoning, or bodily intrusion, the risk may extend to dermatologic injury, medication misuse, dehydration, malnutrition, or repeated emergency visits. The clinician should ask directly about self-treatment, home remedies, weapon carrying, surveillance behavior, confrontation with perceived perpetrators, and any actions taken to "prove" the belief. The more the belief has become operationalized, the more urgent the safety review becomes.

Because shared psychotic disorder is often embedded in a close and sometimes isolated relationship, the safety assessment should not rely solely on what either person says in the room. Collateral information, prior records, and observed interaction patterns are essential for judging whether the situation is stable, escalating, or already dangerous. A calm presentation can mask severe risk if one person is silently complying out of fear or if both have normalized behaviors that would alarm outsiders. The assessment should therefore ask whether either person has access to supportive others, whether they can be separated without immediate destabilization, and whether there is any sign of violence, self-harm, or inability to care for basic needs. In the presence of acute risk, the priority is not diagnostic elegance but immediate protection, containment, and the least restrictive path that still preserves safety.

CHAPTER 6

Chapter 6: Case Studies in Real-World Context

The case material that follows is meant to make the clinical pattern more concrete without turning it into a set of simple formulas. In real settings, shared psychotic disorder rarely looks identical from one relationship to the next; the form it takes depends on temperament, context, stress, and the particular way two lives become organized around the same false certainty. The examples in this chapter therefore move across different relational settings to show how the same underlying process can appear in distinct ways, sometimes through dependence, sometimes through family reinforcement, and sometimes through trust that is difficult to question.

A dependent partner in an isolated relationship

A dependent partner in an isolated relationship often becomes the clearest example of how shared psychotic disorder can take root without dramatic outside visibility. The relationship may look, from the outside, like a private but ordinary partnership: one person is more decisive, more anxious, or more certain; the other is more accommodating, less verbally forceful, and accustomed to deferring. Over time, that difference in style can harden into an imbalance of authority. The more dominant partner begins to define what is real, what is dangerous, and what must be believed. The dependent partner, meanwhile, may come to experience disagreement not as a normal part of intimacy but as a risk to the relationship itself. In that setting, adopting the other person's belief can feel less like surrendering judgment and more like preserving attachment. Isolation intensifies this process by removing the ordinary checks that would otherwise weaken a distorted idea. When a couple lives apart from friends, relatives, coworkers, or community supports, there are fewer opportunities for external reality-testing. A skeptical question from a sibling, a practical observation from a neighbor, or a calm contradiction from a trusted friend can interrupt an unusual belief before it becomes organized into daily life. Without those interruptions, the relationship develops its own closed interpretive system. Events are explained only through the lens the pair shares, and the dependent partner gradually loses access to competing perspectives. In effect, the relationship does not merely contain the belief; it becomes the main environment in which reality is defined.

This kind of dependence is rarely limited to practical matters. It often extends into emotional regulation, decision-making, and identity. The dependent partner may rely on the other person for reassurance, financial stability, social contact, or a sense of purpose. That reliance can make uncertainty feel intolerable. If the dominant partner says a threat is present, or that a suspicious pattern has been uncovered, the dependent person may absorb the claim quickly because it offers structure in a confusing emotional field. The belief may also reduce the discomfort of not knowing. In that sense, the shared delusion is not only an idea; it is a coping arrangement that organizes fear, dependency, and belonging into a single framework.

Clinical descriptions of folie à deux have long noted that transmission is usually most likely where closeness, isolation, and asymmetry converge, rather than where two people simply spend time together [2]. The dependent partner is not necessarily naïve or intellectually impaired. More often, the person is vulnerable because the relationship has trained them to privilege the other person's interpretation over their own. Over repeated interactions, the dominant partner's certainty can function like evidence. Doubt is answered with reassurance, fear is met with more detail, and hesitation is framed as betrayal, weakness, or lack of loyalty. These exchanges create a self-reinforcing loop in which the dependent partner becomes increasingly invested in the shared explanation because rejecting it would also mean challenging the relational order that has formed around it.

What makes the isolated dependent partner especially clinically important is that the belief may appear to be mutually held long before it is truly mutual. The secondary person may echo the dominant partner's language, repeat the same concerns, or begin acting as though the delusion were independently confirmed. Yet this agreement can mask a profound asymmetry in conviction. The dependent partner may still have moments of doubt, but those moments are quickly overridden by fear of conflict, abandonment, or emotional collapse. In practice, the person may appear aligned with the delusion while remaining psychologically organized around the need to maintain closeness. That distinction matters, because it helps explain why the belief can loosen when the relational pressure changes.

In some cases, the dependent partner's participation in the shared belief is also shaped by a narrowed sense of self. When a relationship has become the primary source of identity, the other person's perceptions may be experienced as more trustworthy than one's own internal signals. The result is not simply compliance but a gradual merger of perspectives. The secondary person learns to interpret ambiguity through the dominant partner's emotional tone, to scan for danger in the same places, and to treat contradiction as suspicious. Over time, the relationship can create a kind of borrowed certainty: the dependent partner feels more secure not because the belief is accurate, but because agreement reduces interpersonal tension and preserves the bond.

For clinicians and caregivers, this pattern is important because it can hide in plain sight. A dependent partner in an isolated relationship may seem cooperative, deferential, or even insightful in some settings, while in the company of the dominant partner the same person becomes rigidly aligned with a false belief. That shift is often a clue that the delusion is being maintained relationally rather than simply arising from an independent psychotic process. It also suggests why intervention often has to address both the belief and the structure that supports it. When isolation, dependency, and dominance remain intact, the shared system can continue to regenerate the same conviction even after it has been challenged elsewhere.

A family system shaped by fear and reinforcement

In family settings, shared psychotic disorder often becomes less visible because the household itself begins to function as a closed emotional system. A parent, adult child, sibling pair, or multigenerational unit may organize daily life around one person's fear, suspicion, or certainty, and the rest of the family adapts in ways that seem protective at first. Meals, routines, phone calls, visitors, and even ordinary errands may be filtered through the same concern. The family is not simply "believing" the delusion in a formal sense; it is learning how to live around it. That adaptation can gradually give the false belief the practical authority of fact.

Fear is often the first force that stabilizes the shared system. When a family member is frightened, others may respond with reassurance, vigilance, or compliance, hoping to reduce distress. If the fear is intense enough, the family may decide that questioning it will only make things worse. This is especially likely when one person is seen as fragile, chronically ill, volatile, or psychologically overwhelmed. In that context, disagreement can feel cruel or dangerous. The result is a pattern in which the family's immediate goal becomes emotional containment rather than reality testing. Over time, the false belief gains support not because everyone is convinced, but because everyone is trying to keep the peace.

Reinforcement then turns that peacekeeping into a self-sustaining loop. Each time the family responds as though the delusion might be true, the belief receives confirmation. Avoiding a neighbor, inspecting a room, discarding food, changing locks, or repeatedly discussing the same threat can all function as evidence inside the family's internal logic. Even skeptical relatives may participate indirectly by making accommodations they would never make under ordinary circumstances. The more these behaviors reduce immediate anxiety, the more likely they are to be repeated. What begins as a temporary response to distress becomes a ritualized way of managing daily life. In that sense, the family does not merely witness the delusion; it helps maintain the conditions under which the delusion feels necessary.

In some households, one person becomes the emotional center around which the others organize. That person may be the most fearful, the most controlling, or the most certain, but the key issue is that their interpretation of events sets the tone for the rest of the family. Others may defer because they depend on that person for housing, money, caregiving, or emotional stability. Children can be especially vulnerable in these systems because they often lack the authority or language to challenge what they are taught. Adults may also become dependent when illness, aging, disability, or isolation leaves them with few alternatives. Under those conditions, the family's reality is not negotiated openly; it is inherited through repetition.

High levels of emotional enmeshment make this process harder to interrupt. In an enmeshed family, boundaries between one person's feelings and another's reactions are blurred. A fear expressed by one member is quickly absorbed by the others as if it were shared knowledge rather than a private concern. The family may pride itself on loyalty, unity, or mutual protection, yet that same closeness can reduce the space needed for independent observation. Outsiders may be dismissed as uninformed or intrusive, while internal disagreement is treated as betrayal. When this happens, the family stops functioning as a source of corrective feedback and becomes a closed circuit in which the same belief is echoed, defended, and emotionally amplified.

Authority also matters. In many family cases, the delusional belief is reinforced by a person who has informal power: a parent who controls resources, a spouse who dictates the household atmosphere, or an adult child who has become the family's primary interpreter of events. The family may comply not because the belief is persuasive on its own, but because challenging it would threaten the relationship or invite conflict. This is one reason shared psychosis can become difficult to distinguish from ordinary family stress. The outward behavior may look like accommodation, caregiving, or respect. Clinically, however, the pattern becomes concerning when the family repeatedly sacrifices evidence, perspective, and autonomy in order to preserve one person's account of reality.

Case reports involving family members show how readily shared delusions can take shape in isolated domestic environments, including parent-child and sibling relationships [8][9][2]. Those reports also illustrate an important point: the family system does not need to be overtly chaotic for the problem to deepen. Sometimes it is orderly, dutiful, and highly invested in protecting its own cohesion. That very cohesion can make the delusion harder to challenge because any challenge feels like an attack on the family itself. The belief is then defended not only as true, but as necessary for belonging, safety, or survival. Once that happens, the family is no longer just responding to a symptom; it is living inside a structure organized by fear and reinforcement.

A caregiver relationship complicated by authority and trust

In caregiving relationships, authority can become difficult to separate from trust. The caregiver may have practical control over medication, appointments, transportation, finances, or access to other people, while the dependent person may rely on that same caregiver for reassurance, interpretation, and emotional steadiness. When a shared delusion develops in this context, the relationship can take on a particular rigidity: the caregiver is not only helping with daily needs but also shaping what counts as believable. That influence does not have to be openly coercive to be powerful. It may be expressed through certainty, repeated explanations, or the quiet assumption that the caregiver knows best. Over time, the dependent person may stop comparing the caregiver's account with outside evidence because the relationship itself has become the main lens through which reality is understood.

This pattern is especially concerning when the caregiving role carries institutional or family authority. A parent caring for an adult child, an adult child managing an older parent, or a spouse who has become the primary organizer of daily life may gradually occupy the position of interpreter as well as helper. In that setting, disagreement can feel dangerous because it threatens both practical stability and emotional attachment. The dependent person may fear losing support if they question the caregiver's beliefs, while the caregiver may experience doubt as disloyalty, incompetence, or a refusal to cooperate. The result is a closed loop in which concern is mistaken for proof and compliance is mistaken for understanding. Case literature has described shared delusional processes in family caregiving settings, including parent-child relationships and other close domestic arrangements where the pair is relatively isolated from corrective outside contact [9][2].

Authority also matters because it can disguise itself as responsibility. A caregiver who is managing symptoms, monitoring risks, or advocating in medical settings may genuinely be doing difficult work, and that role can make their interpretations seem especially credible to others. Clinicians, relatives, and service providers may be inclined to defer to the person who appears organized, informed, and protective. If that caregiver is also the source of a delusional framework, the trust placed in them can inadvertently stabilize the belief. The more the environment rewards decisiveness, the less room there is for uncertainty, and uncertainty is often exactly what would allow the dependent person to pause, reflect, and compare perspectives.

This is one reason shared psychotic disorder in caregiving contexts can be hard to identify early. The relationship may look devoted rather than distorted. A caregiver may speak in the language of advocacy, vigilance, or protection while gradually narrowing the dependent person's access to alternative explanations. Calls to relatives may be filtered, appointments may be framed in a single direction, and outside disagreement may be dismissed as misunderstanding or neglect. In some cases, even when the belief is bizarre or medically implausible, the caregiving role gives it a practical cover: "I am only trying to keep them safe." That framing can make it difficult for others to distinguish legitimate concern from a relational system that has begun to organize itself around a false conviction.

The imbalance becomes more visible when the caregiver controls not only information but also consequences. If the dependent person questions the belief, does the caregiver withdraw support, become angry, or increase monitoring? Does the person being cared for appear calmer when separated from the caregiver, only to become more convinced after repeated exposure? These are clinically important questions because they reveal whether the belief is being maintained by dependence rather than by evidence. In some reported cases of shared psychosis, the secondary person's conviction has weakened once contact with the inducing figure was reduced, underscoring how strongly the relationship itself can sustain the delusion [1][4].

Trust complicates intervention as well. A dependent person may not experience the caregiver as controlling, even when outside observers do. They may describe the caregiver as the only one who understands what is happening or the only person willing to take the problem seriously. For that reason, direct confrontation can backfire if it is experienced as an attack on the relationship. The clinical task is often to assess how much of the belief is held because it feels true and how much is held because it preserves attachment, safety, or access to care. That distinction matters because a person may be willing to question the belief only when they can imagine that doing so will not destroy the bond that keeps daily life functioning.

In the most difficult cases, the caregiving role becomes a source of both genuine need and psychological risk. The dependent person may truly require assistance, and the caregiver may truly be overwhelmed, frightened, or isolated. Yet the same conditions that make caregiving necessary can also make shared delusion more durable: limited outside contact, high stress, role asymmetry, and a growing reliance on one another for reality testing. Clinically, this means the relationship cannot be evaluated only by asking who is "right." It must also be understood as a system in which authority, dependence, and emotional trust may have fused so tightly that the delusion is sustained by the very structure of care.

Lessons learned from recovery, relapse, and treatment response

Recovery from shared psychotic disorder rarely follows a clean, linear path. In many cases, the first meaningful change is not the disappearance of the belief itself, but a shift in the relationship that has been sustaining it. When contact is reduced, when outside support becomes available, or when the more dominant person is no longer reinforcing the delusion, the secondary person may begin to test reality in small, uneven ways. That process can look fragile from the outside: a person may alternate between doubt and conviction, insight and defensiveness, relief and fear. Clinically, those fluctuations are important. They show that the shared belief is not simply a fixed idea, but something that has been held in place by interpersonal pressure, emotional dependence, and repeated confirmation.

One of the clearest lessons from recovery is that improvement in the secondary person does not always mean the original belief was never deeply held. It may mean that the relational conditions supporting the belief have changed enough for doubt to become tolerable again. In some cases, separation from the primary person leads to rapid softening of the delusion; in others, the person remains convinced for a longer period, especially if the belief has become tied to identity, fear, or a sense of loyalty. Reports in the literature describe cases in which shared delusional beliefs improved after the relationship was disrupted and treatment was introduced, but the timing and degree of response varied widely [1][2][4]. That variability is a reminder that the disorder is not governed by a single mechanism and cannot be managed with a single expectation.

Relapse often appears when the old interpersonal pattern reasserts itself. A person who has gained some distance may begin to drift back into the same belief if contact resumes under the same emotional conditions, especially if the relationship again becomes isolated, controlling, or organized around fear. This is why relapse prevention has to focus on more than symptom monitoring. It also has to track the structure of daily life: who has influence, who is providing reality checks, whether outside relationships have been restored, and whether the person is once again being pulled into a closed system of interpretation. In family-based presentations, the return of the same routines, the same conversations, and the same mutual reinforcement can recreate the original conditions with surprising speed [9].

Treatment response is often strongest when the intervention matches the level of entanglement. If the secondary person is still living inside the same relational field as the primary person, individual reassurance alone may not be enough. The person may need a combination of separation, psychiatric evaluation, and carefully paced psychotherapy that does not directly attack the belief in a confrontational way. When symptoms are severe, medication may be useful as part of a broader plan, especially if there is comorbid anxiety, depression, or a primary psychotic disorder in one of the involved individuals [7][2]. In some reported cases, low-dose antipsychotic treatment was associated with clinical improvement when the delusional framework had become entrenched and distressing [7].

Another lesson is that the person with the shared belief may not experience the change as “treatment” at first. They may experience it as betrayal, coercion, humiliation, or abandonment. If clinicians or family members move too quickly, the person may cling more tightly to the belief as a way of preserving autonomy or relationship loyalty. This is especially true when the delusion has been woven into a caregiving or dependency dynamic. In those situations, response to treatment is often better when the approach protects dignity, avoids public confrontation, and gives the person a face-saving path toward reconsidering what they believe. The goal is not to force immediate confession or agreement, but to make room for enough psychological safety that reality testing can return.

Recovery also teaches that insight can arrive in fragments. A person may first admit that the situation feels less certain, then later recognize that they acted on fear, and only afterward fully question the original belief. Those stages matter because they show that recovery is not identical with instant disbelief. It may involve rebuilding confidence in one's own perceptions, learning to tolerate uncertainty, and separating personal identity from the shared narrative. In the best outcomes, the person is not simply "talked out of" a delusion; they regain the ability to compare impressions, consult others, and make decisions without needing the relationship to certify reality.

For clinicians and caregivers, the practical implication is that response should be judged across several domains at once: the intensity of the belief, the degree of behavioral change, the quality of the relationship, and the person's ability to function outside the shared system. A partial response may still be clinically meaningful if it reduces risk, restores sleep or eating, lowers agitation, or opens the door to outside support. Conversely, a person may appear calmer while remaining fully embedded in the delusion, which is why surface improvement alone can be misleading. The most durable recoveries tend to occur when the relationship no longer rewards the belief, when the person has access to independent support, and when treatment addresses both the symptom and the social setting that allowed it to spread [6][8][3].

CHAPTER 7

Chapter 7: Treatment Principles and Clinical Intervention

Once a shared delusion has begun to shape daily life, treatment has to address more than the belief itself; it has to reduce immediate risk, interrupt the relational conditions that keep the belief alive, and create enough stability for careful clinical work to begin. In practice, that means the first phase of intervention is often less about persuasion than about containment, clarity, and coordinated support. Clinicians may need to move deliberately, because the people involved may be frightened, distrustful, or highly invested in preserving the shared framework that has organized their relationship.

Initial stabilization and safety planning

Initial stabilization begins with the most immediate question: what needs to be made safer right now so that assessment and treatment can happen at all? In shared psychotic disorder, the people involved may not arrive asking for help with a shared delusion. They may present with anxiety, conflict, insomnia, agitation, suspiciousness, refusal of care, or a crisis that has already escalated into threats, self-harm, medical neglect, or attempts to confront an imagined source of danger. The first task is therefore not to challenge the belief directly, but to reduce the conditions that are making the situation volatile. That often means slowing the pace of interaction, separating people when needed, and identifying who is most at risk of acting on the belief in the next hours or days.

Safety planning has to be concrete. Vague reassurance is not enough when a delusional framework is driving behavior. The clinician needs to ask whether either person has access to weapons, medications, sharp objects, or other means that could be used impulsively; whether there have been threats toward self or others; whether the belief is leading to refusal of food, water, sleep, or necessary medical treatment; and whether the relationship itself is preventing honest reporting of risk. In some cases, the secondary person appears less distressed but is more likely to follow the primary person's instructions, including dangerous ones. In others, the primary person is frightened and unstable, while the secondary person has become the one most likely to act. The plan has to account for the actual pattern of influence, not just the diagnostic labels.

When the shared belief centers on persecution, contamination, infestation, poisoning, surveillance, or spiritual attack, the risk often comes from defensive behavior. People may barricade themselves, discard belongings, confront neighbors, damage property, or refuse to leave a location they believe is protected. Delusional infestation is a common example of how fixed false beliefs can produce escalating distress and self-directed harm, including skin picking, repeated cleansing, or urgent medical demands despite negative findings [5]. In these situations, stabilization may require practical steps that seem modest but are clinically important: limiting access to tools used for self-injury, arranging sleep and nutrition, reducing confrontation, and helping the person postpone irreversible decisions until they are calmer and more fully evaluated.

Separation is sometimes necessary, but it should be done thoughtfully. If the relationship is highly enmeshed, continued contact can keep the belief active through repetition and mutual reassurance. Yet abrupt separation without support can intensify panic, especially if one person depends on the other for orientation or daily functioning. A safer approach is often structured distance: temporary physical separation, supervised contact, or different points of contact for each person so that one account does not immediately reinforce the other. In family settings, this may include identifying a neutral relative, case manager, shelter provider, or inpatient team member who can help coordinate communication without validating the delusion. The goal is to interrupt the feedback loop while preserving enough stability to avoid unnecessary escalation.

Medication decisions belong to the broader stabilization picture, even when the immediate focus is safety rather than definitive diagnosis. If agitation, insomnia, severe anxiety, or psychotic intensity is interfering with functioning, psychiatric consultation may be needed quickly. The presence of shared psychotic symptoms does not rule out a primary psychotic disorder, mood disorder with psychotic features, substance-related condition, or medical cause, and the level of acuity may require treatment before the picture can be fully clarified [1][2]. At the same time, clinicians should avoid framing medication as proof that the belief is “all in the mind.” For some patients, the first useful message is simply that the treatment is aimed at helping them sleep, think more clearly, and feel less overwhelmed while the team evaluates what is happening.

Because the relationship itself is often part of the risk, safety planning should include communication boundaries. Caregivers and family members may need explicit guidance not to argue, ridicule, or repeatedly investigate the delusion in ways that intensify it. They also need to know what to do if the person becomes more distressed, more suspicious, or more intent on acting. A written crisis plan can be helpful: who to call, when to seek emergency evaluation, which statements are useful, which topics should be avoided, and what changes signal that the situation is moving from concerning to urgent. This is especially important when one person is isolated from outside feedback, since the absence of alternative perspectives can make the delusional system more durable [9].

In the earliest phase, stabilization is often measured by small but meaningful gains: a person agrees to eat, sleep, or accept an evaluation; a pair agrees to separate temporarily; a family agrees to stop reinforcing a dangerous routine; or a caregiver agrees to hand over control of a specific decision. Those changes may not resolve the belief, but they create enough safety for treatment to proceed. In shared psychotic disorder, that is not a minor achievement. It is the point at which the relationship begins to loosen its hold just enough for reality testing, risk assessment, and longer-term intervention to become possible.

Psychotherapy approaches for the affected individuals

Psychotherapy with affected individuals has to be paced to the person's level of insight, emotional dependence, and current safety. The first task is rarely direct confrontation. If treatment begins by attacking the belief too forcefully, the clinician may be experienced as another threatening outsider, and the person may retreat further into the shared system for reassurance. A more effective stance is calm, respectful, and steady: the therapist acknowledges distress, explores the person's experience in detail, and avoids validating the delusion itself. This approach helps preserve engagement while creating enough distance for reflection to begin.

Individual psychotherapy is often most useful when it focuses on the consequences of the belief before it focuses on the belief's truth value. Sleep disruption, hypervigilance, conflict, shame, social withdrawal, and impaired functioning are often easier entry points than the delusion's content. By working with these concrete problems, the therapist can help the person regain a sense of agency without forcing an immediate ideological battle. In practice, this may include helping the person notice patterns of escalation, identifying moments when fear intensifies, and examining how certain interactions make the belief feel more convincing. The goal is not to argue the person out of the delusion in a single session, but to widen the space in which alternative interpretations can be considered.

Supportive psychotherapy is especially important when the secondary person has been living inside a relationship that has narrowed their autonomy. Many affected individuals have spent so long adapting to another person's certainty that they have lost confidence in their own judgment. Therapy can help restore that confidence by reinforcing independent thinking, emotional regulation, and reality-testing skills. The therapist may ask the person to describe events in sequence, compare interpretations, and notice the difference between a feeling of certainty and external evidence. These interventions are often subtle, but they matter because they rebuild the capacity to pause before endorsing a shared belief.

When the person is able to tolerate more structured work, cognitive approaches can be adapted to the clinical picture. The aim is not to challenge every unusual statement, but to help the person examine how conclusions are formed and maintained. A therapist might explore what evidence the person notices, what evidence is ignored, and how fear shapes perception. In some cases, gentle behavioral experiments are possible, especially when the person is already beginning to question the shared belief. These experiments should be collaborative and low-risk, designed to test assumptions in ordinary life rather than provoke embarrassment or escalation. The emphasis remains on curiosity, not confrontation.

Because shared psychotic disorder is relational by nature, psychotherapy often has to address the person's attachment patterns and interpersonal dependence as directly as the belief itself. If the secondary person has come to rely on the dominant individual for identity, safety, or decision-making, then separation from the delusional framework may feel like emotional abandonment. Therapy can make that dependency explicit without shaming it. The clinician may help the person identify what the relationship provides, what it costs, and what fears arise when independent thought is introduced. Over time, this work can support healthier boundaries, improved self-trust, and a more stable sense of self that is not organized around another person's certainty.

In some cases, family or couple work becomes necessary, but it must be used carefully. Joint sessions can be helpful when they reduce secrecy, improve communication, and allow the clinician to observe relational dynamics in real time. They can also be counterproductive if the more dominant person uses the session to reinforce the delusion, control the narrative, or pressure the other person into agreement. For that reason, the therapist has to assess whether conjoint treatment will support reality-testing or simply reproduce the same relational hierarchy. When joint work is appropriate, the focus should remain on safety, communication, and functioning rather than on deciding who is "right" about the delusional content.

Therapy also has to account for the possibility that the affected person is not fully ready to separate from the shared belief. Ambivalence is common. A person may partially doubt the delusion and still feel terrified of losing the relationship or the structure it provides. In that setting, motivational work can be valuable. The therapist can explore the person's goals—sleeping better, reducing conflict, returning to work, reconnecting with family, feeling less afraid—and show how those goals may be blocked by the current pattern. This keeps treatment anchored in the person's own priorities rather than in abstract diagnostic correction.

The psychotherapy process is usually slow, uneven, and dependent on the broader environment. If the person continues to be isolated, monitored, or pressured by the other party, progress may be limited. If the relationship begins to loosen and outside supports become available, therapy can become much more effective. Even then, setbacks are common, especially when stress rises or contact with the reinforcing person resumes. The therapeutic task is therefore not simply to eliminate a false belief, but to help the affected individual recover enough psychological independence to evaluate experience with less fear and more freedom.

Medication, comorbidity, and psychiatric consultation

Medication is not the primary treatment for shared psychotic disorder itself, but it often becomes relevant because the clinical picture rarely exists in isolation. When a shared delusion is active, one or both people may also be dealing with anxiety, insomnia, major depression, trauma-related symptoms, substance use, or a primary psychotic disorder that predates the relationship. In those situations, medication may be used to treat the comorbid condition, reduce agitation, improve sleep, or stabilize a broader psychotic process. The goal is not to "medicate away" the relationship dynamic; it is to address the symptoms and vulnerabilities that are keeping the system unstable.

This distinction matters because medication response can be misleading if it is interpreted too narrowly. A person may become calmer on an antipsychotic or antidepressant and still hold the same shared belief, especially if the relational environment remains unchanged. Conversely, a reduction in distress may make the person more willing to question the belief, even if the delusional content has not disappeared. In practice, medication is most useful when it supports a larger treatment plan rather than standing in for one. That plan usually includes careful observation of both individuals, attention to safety, and a realistic understanding that symptom relief may be partial before it is sustained.

Comorbidity is common enough to require deliberate assessment. A clinician should consider whether the shared belief is occurring alongside schizophrenia spectrum illness, delusional disorder, bipolar disorder with psychotic features, severe depression, obsessive-compulsive symptoms with poor insight, post-traumatic stress, neurocognitive decline, or substance-induced psychosis. In some cases, the secondary person's symptoms fade when separated from the primary person, while in others the secondary person reveals an independent disorder that needs its own treatment. That is one reason the diagnostic process cannot stop at the relational pattern alone. The apparent "shared" quality may obscure a second condition that is clinically significant in its own right.

Medication decisions should therefore be tied to the question of who is being treated for what. If one person has a clear primary psychotic disorder, mood disorder, or severe agitation, pharmacologic treatment may be indicated on standard psychiatric grounds. If the other person is mainly distressed, sleep-deprived, or anxious but does not show a separate psychotic illness, medication may be short term and symptom focused. In either case, the prescriber has to watch for medication adherence problems that arise from mistrust, dependency, coercion, or the shared belief itself. A person who believes the treatment team is part of the threat may refuse medication, hide side effects, or take doses inconsistently. The clinical response has to be calm, transparent, and coordinated rather than confrontational.

Psychiatric consultation becomes especially important when the presentation is diagnostically unclear, medically complicated, or potentially dangerous. Consultation can help sort out whether the symptoms are better explained by a primary psychotic disorder, a mood disorder, a neurologic condition, intoxication, withdrawal, or a relationally sustained delusion. It is also valuable when there is uncertainty about capacity, involuntary treatment, medication risk, or the need for hospitalization. In shared psychotic disorder, the stakes can rise quickly if the belief is prompting self-neglect, aggression, refusal of needed medical care, or attempts to act on the delusion. A psychiatric consultant can help determine whether the immediate priority is stabilization, separation, medication initiation, or a broader multidisciplinary response.

The consultation process should also account for the fact that both people may present with partial insight and strong interpersonal loyalty. A secondary person may appear less impaired simply because the delusion is less elaborate or less fixed, yet still be highly vulnerable to reinforcement. A primary person may have a more established psychotic illness that has drawn the other person into its orbit. These differences affect medication strategy. For example, one person may need ongoing antipsychotic treatment while the other benefits more from short-term symptomatic support and structured psychotherapy. Bernal-Rocha and colleagues describe a marital case in which the shared psychosis dynamic was sustained within the family relationship, underscoring how tightly symptom expression can remain linked to the interpersonal setting [11].

It is also important to monitor for side effects and iatrogenic complications, especially when the patient's trust in treatment is fragile. Sedation, akathisia, weight gain, sexual side effects, and cognitive dulling can all reduce adherence and deepen suspicion. If the person already feels controlled by others, an unpleasant medication experience may be interpreted as further evidence of persecution or manipulation. That makes follow-up essential. The prescriber should explain the purpose of the medication in plain language, review expected benefits and risks, and invite reporting of side effects early rather than waiting for the patient to disengage.

In many cases, the most effective psychiatric consultation is not a one-time diagnostic opinion but an ongoing collaboration with therapists, primary care clinicians, family members when appropriate, and social supports. Shared psychotic disorder often sits at the boundary between psychiatry and relationship systems, which means medication decisions have to be revisited as the relational context changes. If separation occurs, if the more dominant person is hospitalized, or if the secondary person gains outside support, medication needs may change as well. The prescriber's task is to remain anchored in the evolving clinical picture rather than assuming that the first formulation will remain true throughout treatment.

Coordinating care across family, medical, and social supports

Coordination works best when it is treated as a structured clinical task rather than an informal effort to "keep everyone on the same page." In shared psychotic disorder, the same relationship that sustains the delusion can also block useful help, so the care plan has to account for multiple systems at once: the family or close relationship, the medical team, and the broader social supports that can widen perspective without escalating conflict. The goal is not to create a single unified narrative at all costs. It is to reduce isolation, improve safety, and make sure that each part of the system is responding to the same clinical reality.

At the family level, coordination begins with clarity about roles. One person may be the primary contact for appointments, another may be handling transportation, and a third may be most likely to observe day-to-day changes. When those roles are undefined, the result is often confusion, mixed messages, or accidental reinforcement of the shared belief. It is usually more effective to decide in advance who will communicate with clinicians, who will monitor medication adherence or side effects, and who will notice changes in sleep, agitation, self-care, or suspiciousness. This is especially important when the relationship itself is part of the problem, because the person most emotionally entangled in the delusion may also be the least able to provide neutral observations.

Medical coordination should be grounded in a shared understanding of what is being treated. One clinician may be addressing a primary psychotic disorder, another may be managing anxiety, insomnia, trauma symptoms, or a medical complaint that has become wrapped into the delusional system. If these pieces are handled separately, the result can be fragmented care that unintentionally strengthens uncertainty. Clear communication between psychiatry, primary care, and any relevant specialty services helps prevent unnecessary testing, repeated reassurance cycles, or contradictory explanations. This is particularly important in presentations that resemble somatic or infestation-related delusions, where repeated medical visits can become part of the reinforcement pattern if the underlying psychiatric dynamics are not recognized [5].

In practice, the most useful medical coordination is often conservative and consistent. Clinicians should agree on how to discuss symptoms, which concerns require urgent reassessment, and how to respond when the patient returns with the same belief in a heightened form. A measured approach reduces the chance that one provider will validate the delusion while another tries to challenge it aggressively. It also helps the patient experience the system as stable rather than adversarial. In cases where the clinical picture includes risk, agitation, or severe distress, coordinated medication management and follow-up can be essential to maintaining enough stability for the relationship to loosen its grip [7].

Social supports matter because shared psychotic disorder often thrives where outside contact has been reduced. Friends, relatives, case managers, peer supporters, faith leaders, and community services can all serve as reality-testing influences, but only if their role is carefully chosen. The point is not to flood the person with dissenting opinions. Too much confrontation can lead to withdrawal and greater reliance on the shared belief. Instead, the aim is to restore ordinary, low-pressure contact with people who can offer structure, practical help, and a wider frame of reference. Even brief, regular contact with a trusted outsider may interrupt the closed loop of the relationship and lower the emotional intensity that keeps the belief alive [9].

When social services are involved, coordination should be specific and documented. If housing instability, financial dependence, domestic conflict, or caregiving overload are part of the picture, those stressors need attention alongside the psychiatric symptoms. A case manager may help with appointment adherence, benefits, transportation, or linkage to community programs; a social worker may help assess whether the living arrangement itself is sustaining the delusion. In family-based presentations, especially those involving more than two people, the system may have adapted so thoroughly that each person's behavior appears reasonable in isolation [8]. Care coordination has to look at the pattern as a whole, not just the most vocal individual.

One of the most delicate tasks is deciding how much information can be shared across settings. Confidentiality still matters, but so does safety. If the patient consents, it is often helpful to involve family members or other supports in treatment planning, psychoeducation, and relapse monitoring. If consent is limited, clinicians can still gather collateral information and provide general guidance without disclosing unnecessary details. The key is to avoid creating secrecy around a dangerous belief while also avoiding disclosures that could intensify mistrust. In high-control relationships, careful boundary setting may be the first step toward making outside support usable at all [2].

Coordinated care also benefits from a simple crisis plan that everyone understands. That plan should identify early warning signs, specify whom to call if the person becomes more agitated or begins acting on the belief, and clarify when emergency evaluation is needed. It should also name which responses are unhelpful, such as arguing about the delusion, repeatedly seeking reassurance, or allowing the shared belief to dictate every household decision. When family, medical, and social supports are aligned around the same practical steps, the person affected by the delusion is less likely to experience each contact as a separate battle. Instead, the system begins to function as a steady external anchor while treatment takes hold.

CHAPTER 8

Chapter 8: Supporting Families, Caregivers, and Loved Ones

For families and caregivers, the central challenge is not only what to believe, but how to remain steady when another person's certainty begins to organize the household. In shared psychotic disorder, loved ones are often pulled into a difficult position: they may want to comfort, calm, or protect, yet every response risks either reinforcing the delusion or deepening conflict. That tension can make ordinary conversations feel charged and every decision feel consequential. The work ahead, then, is less about winning an argument than about preserving safety, clarity, and connection without surrendering to the false framework that is shaping the relationship.

How to respond without validating delusions

The most useful responses begin with a discipline that is easy to describe and difficult to maintain: acknowledge the person's distress without affirming the delusion as fact. That means answering the feeling, not the false belief. If someone says, "They are putting something in my food," a response such as "That sounds frightening, and I can see you feel unsafe" recognizes the emotion while leaving the claim unendorsed. This approach avoids the two extremes that often make matters worse: direct agreement, which can deepen the shared system, and blunt contradiction, which can trigger defensiveness, shame, or escalation. In practice, the goal is not to win an argument about reality. It is to remain connected enough that the person can keep talking and, over time, remain reachable.

This kind of response depends on careful wording. Phrases like "I believe you" or "You're right" may feel compassionate in the moment, but they can inadvertently validate the delusion itself. At the same time, saying "That's not true" or "You're imagining it" may be experienced as dismissive or hostile, especially when the person's sense of safety is already fragile. More effective language stays close to observable experience: "You seem very upset," "I want to understand what you're going through," "I don't see evidence of that, but I do see that this is affecting you," or "Let's focus on what would help you feel safer right now." Such statements neither intensify the belief nor abandon the person to it. They preserve dignity while quietly holding a boundary around reality.

When the belief is shared within a relationship, the response has to account for the interpersonal pattern as much as the content. A caregiver, partner, or family member may feel pressure to choose sides, especially if the dominant person is highly insistent. Yet taking a side usually strengthens the closed loop. Instead, it is often better to avoid debating the details with either person and to redirect attention toward concrete needs: sleep, food, hydration, medical evaluation, daily structure, and emotional regulation. If the delusion involves contamination, surveillance, infestation, poisoning, or persecution, practical support can sound like, "Let's check what is actually happening with the apartment," or "We can talk to a doctor about the symptoms you're noticing." This keeps the conversation anchored in action rather than in confirming the imagined cause.

It is also important to resist the urge to gather evidence in a way that becomes part of the delusion. Repeated reassurance can become a ritual that temporarily calms anxiety while reinforcing the false framework. So can excessive investigation, checking, or protective behavior if it is framed as proof that the feared event is real. The better course is to set a calm limit: "I'm not able to help confirm that theory, but I am willing to help you with the discomfort, the appointment, or the next safe step." In cases where the person seeks constant reassurance, a predictable response is often more helpful than a highly emotional one. Consistency communicates steadiness, and steadiness can matter more than persuasion.

Nonverbal behavior matters as much as language. Tone should be calm, even, and respectful; facial expressions should not signal ridicule or alarm. Sudden changes in volume, sarcasm, whispering, or visible disbelief can be interpreted as betrayal and may intensify suspicion. If the person is agitated, it helps to reduce stimulation, slow the pace of the interaction, and keep the conversation brief and concrete. Offering choices can also reduce power struggles: "Would you rather talk now or after you've had some water?" "Do you want to sit here or in the other room?" Small choices restore a sense of agency without conceding the delusion. In many cases, preserving the relationship is the more immediate clinical task, because a person who feels cornered is less likely to accept any help at all.

Family members and caregivers often need permission to stop arguing. They may have been told, implicitly or explicitly, that if they just found the right explanation, the belief would collapse. But shared delusions do not usually yield to logic delivered under stress. A more realistic aim is to avoid feeding the belief while still attending to the person's emotional state and safety. That may mean repeating a limited set of responses, refusing to participate in escalating certainty, and gently steering the conversation away from the delusional content when possible. In some settings, especially where the relationship has become highly controlling or coercive, even well-meant reassurance can be used to recruit others into the delusional framework [9][10].

There are moments when the safest response is not deeper discussion but prompt escalation to professional help. If the person is refusing food, medication, or medical care because of the belief; if they are threatening themselves or someone else; or if the delusion is driving dangerous behavior, the priority shifts from communication technique to urgent assessment. Even then, the principle remains the same: do not validate the delusion in order to keep the peace. Instead, acknowledge the distress, state the boundary, and move toward concrete support. The message is simple and steady: "I can see this is serious, and I want to help you get the right care." That stance protects both the person's trust and the clinician's or caregiver's ability to respond without becoming part of the false reality.

Setting boundaries and reducing enabling behaviors

Setting boundaries begins with recognizing that support is not the same as participation. A family member or caregiver can remain compassionate without becoming an extension of the delusion. In practice, this means deciding in advance what kinds of conversations, requests, and behaviors can be met with reassurance, what must be redirected, and what will not be negotiated. If the person insists on a false belief, the goal is not to win an argument but to avoid feeding the belief with repeated confirmation, investigation, or ritualized checking. The more a household organizes itself around proving, disproving, or managing the delusion, the more the belief can become the center of daily life.

Boundaries are most effective when they are concrete and behavior-based. Vague statements such as "I can't do this anymore" often collapse under pressure because they do not specify what will change. Clearer limits sound more like: "I will talk with you about how scared you feel, but I will not call the police unless there is an actual emergency," or "I can drive you to an appointment, but I will not help you confront the neighbor." This kind of language avoids shaming and keeps the focus on actions. It also helps the unaffected person stay consistent, which matters because inconsistency can be interpreted as permission to keep escalating demands. In some cases, especially when paranoia or infestation beliefs are involved, even well-meant participation in repeated inspections, cleaning, or reassurance can reinforce the cycle and should be reduced carefully [5].

Reducing enabling behaviors usually requires identifying the small ways a system has adapted to the delusion. Enabling is not always obvious. It may look like answering the same question twenty times a day, rearranging routines to avoid imagined danger, hiding information to prevent distress, or taking over tasks the person can still manage because it is easier than facing conflict. These responses often come from love, fear, or exhaustion, but they can unintentionally communicate that the belief deserves special status. Over time, the affected person may depend less on reality testing and more on the family's accommodations. A healthier pattern is to meet genuine needs directly while refusing to build the household around the false belief. That may mean helping with sleep, meals, transport, or medical care while declining to participate in avoidance rituals or repeated reassurance seeking.

It is also important to reduce the social conditions that make enabling easier. Isolation tends to intensify shared delusions, so boundaries should not become another form of confinement. The unaffected person may need to widen the circle of contact by encouraging outside appointments, regular routines, and safe relationships that are not organized around the delusion. That can include involving a clinician, primary care provider, case manager, or trusted relative who can offer a steadier perspective. In family cases, especially where multiple people have begun to adapt to the same fear, a more open structure can interrupt the closed feedback loop that keeps the belief alive [8][9]. The aim is not to flood the person with contradictory opinions, but to restore access to ordinary reality checks.

When the shared belief is tied to authority or dependency, boundary-setting may feel risky because the more dominant person can react with anger, withdrawal, or accusations of betrayal. In those situations, the caregiver or family member should avoid making boundaries contingent on the other person's agreement. A boundary is not a debate; it is a statement about what the helper will and will not do. If the person becomes hostile, the response should stay brief and calm: "I hear that you're upset. I'm not able to do that." Repeating the same limit without elaboration often works better than defending it. Long explanations can become another opening for argument, while steady repetition communicates predictability. If there is a history of coercion, intimidation, or retaliation, boundaries may need to be paired with a safety plan and outside professional guidance.

Reducing enabling also means tolerating the distress that may follow when the old pattern no longer holds. People who have been caught in a shared delusional system often experience guilt when they stop accommodating, as if they are abandoning the person or making the situation worse. In reality, the initial increase in anger, pleading, or insistence may reflect the loss of reinforcement rather than proof that the boundary is wrong. The helper's task is to remain supportive without becoming absorbed into the delusion's logic. That can include validating emotion, offering practical help, and refusing to endorse the false claim. If the person's behavior becomes unsafe, if there is self-harm, threats, refusal of essential care, or escalating confrontation, the boundary shifts from relational preference to urgent clinical concern [7].

In many households, the most useful boundary is a shared agreement about what the family will no longer do together. That may mean no more group discussions about the delusion after a certain point, no more late-night reassurance cycles, no more checking the same fear over and over, and no more private codes that keep the belief socially protected. These limits work best when they are paired with a clear alternative: a clinician to contact, a calming routine to use, a place to step away, or a neutral activity that does not revolve around the feared idea. The purpose is not to force insight by pressure. It is to make room for a different relational environment—one in which care remains available, but the delusion no longer directs every response.

Recognizing when to seek urgent professional intervention

Urgent professional intervention becomes necessary when the shared belief is no longer just unusual or distressing, but is actively driving danger, loss of control, or an inability to care for basic needs. In practice, the threshold is not whether the belief sounds implausible to outside observers; it is whether the people involved are acting in ways that could reasonably lead to harm. That harm may be immediate, as when someone is threatening self-injury, refusing essential medical care, or preparing to confront a perceived enemy. It may also be slower and less visible, as when sleep, nutrition, hygiene, work, parenting, or medication adherence are steadily collapsing under the pressure of the delusion.

One of the clearest warning signs is the presence of suicidal thinking, self-harm, or statements that life is no longer bearable because of the shared belief. A person may say they would rather die than continue being watched, poisoned, contaminated, or controlled. They may also become hopeless after repeated efforts to "fix" the imagined problem fail. In some cases, the distress is tied to physical sensations or bodily fears, as in delusional infestation, where the person becomes increasingly preoccupied with symptoms and may escalate to unsafe skin-picking, chemical use, or repeated emergency visits [5]. When suicidal language appears, it should always be treated as urgent, even if the person seems calm or the belief itself has been present for a long time.

Another red flag is a rapid increase in agitation, paranoia, or defensive behavior that narrows the person's options. If the individual begins carrying weapons, barricading doors, confronting strangers, making repeated reports to authorities, or refusing to leave home because of a perceived threat, the situation has moved beyond a conversational problem. The same is true when the shared belief starts to justify aggression toward a spouse, relative, neighbor, clinician, or perceived persecutor. What matters here is not only the intensity of the conviction, but the way it is reorganizing behavior toward confrontation. Shared delusional systems can become especially risky when one person's certainty gives the other permission to act on fear.

Urgent intervention is also warranted when the relationship itself is becoming coercive or unstable enough that the secondary person cannot think independently. If one person is controlling access to phones, transportation, money, medication, or outside contact, the shared belief may be embedded in a broader pattern of domination. In those circumstances, the problem is not simply that two people agree on a false idea; it is that the more dependent person may have no safe way to test reality or seek help. A clinician, family member, or caregiver should be especially concerned if the secondary person appears frightened to disagree, speaks in the other person's language, or seems unable to answer questions without checking for approval.

Immediate professional help is also needed when functioning falls sharply. Missing work, neglecting children, not eating, not sleeping, abandoning medical treatment, or failing to manage basic household tasks can all signal that the delusion is taking priority over survival needs. The same concern applies when the person is repeatedly seeking unnecessary medical treatment for a fixed false belief, especially if they are becoming more distressed despite reassurance and negative findings. In some cases, the presentation resembles a psychotic disorder with shared features rather than a stable, contained delusion, and the risk profile may be higher than it first appears [1][2]. A sudden change from eccentricity to disorganization should never be minimized.

Families and caregivers should also seek urgent intervention if there is any uncertainty about the person's ability to remain safe overnight or through the next day. That includes threats to leave home impulsively, drive while highly agitated, confront someone believed to be dangerous, or take medications in unsafe ways. If children, older adults, or medically vulnerable people are in the environment, the threshold for action should be lower. A household can become dangerous long before anyone is formally injured, especially when fear, sleeplessness, and mutual reinforcement have made the shared belief feel like the only reality that matters. Cases involving close family members show how quickly the condition can intensify when isolation and emotional dependence are present [9].

When immediate danger is possible, the correct response is not prolonged debate. Emergency services, crisis teams, urgent psychiatric evaluation, or the nearest emergency department may be appropriate depending on the severity of the situation and local resources. If the person has already made a suicide threat, attempted self-harm, become physically aggressive, or is unable to care for basic needs, the situation should be treated as a crisis. In clinical settings, emergency presentation is often what finally interrupts a deteriorating pattern, especially when the person has become unreachable through ordinary reassurance or outpatient discussion [7]. For caregivers, the practical rule is simple: if you are asking whether this can wait, and there is credible risk of harm, it probably should not wait.

In the moment, it helps to focus on safety rather than persuading the person that the belief is false. Keep the interaction brief, calm, and concrete. Remove access to weapons, sharp objects, large quantities of medication, or anything else that could be used impulsively. If possible, stay with the person or ensure that another responsible adult is present until help arrives. If the person is resistant, do not escalate into an argument about the delusion; instead, emphasize concern for distress, sleep, physical safety, and the need for immediate support. The goal is not to win the discussion. The goal is to prevent the next harmful action long enough for professional care to take over.

Supporting the unaffected person and the broader family system

Supporting the person who has not adopted the delusion requires a careful balance of protection and respect. That person may be living in the same emotional weather as everyone else in the household, yet their experience is often overlooked because attention naturally centers on the more symptomatic or more disruptive individual. The unaffected person may be confused, ashamed, frightened, or quietly worn down by the need to keep peace. They may also feel responsible for holding the relationship together, especially if they have spent months or years trying to compensate for instability, calm repeated crises, or prevent escalation. In clinical work, it is important to recognize that this person is not simply a bystander. They are often the one most able to notice changes early, but they may also be the one least free to speak plainly.

One of the most useful interventions is to restore the unaffected person's confidence in their own perceptions. Shared psychotic disorder can create a kind of interpersonal pressure in which doubt is treated as disloyalty and outside perspective is framed as misunderstanding. Over time, the unaffected person may begin to second-guess ordinary observations, especially if they have been repeatedly told that their concerns are exaggerated or that they "do not understand what is really happening." Clinicians and caregivers can help by naming this erosion directly and calmly. The goal is not to convince the person that every concern they have is correct, but to strengthen their ability to notice, compare, and question without immediately surrendering their own judgment to the dominant narrative.

That support often includes making space for private conversations. When the unaffected person can speak without being monitored, interrupted, or corrected by the other party, they are more likely to describe the relationship accurately. They may reveal patterns that are hard to see in the presence of the delusional system: chronic fear of conflict, financial dependence, sleep disruption, pressure to agree, or a growing sense that their life has narrowed around someone else's beliefs. Private contact also allows the clinician to assess whether the person is merely distressed by the situation or is themselves becoming psychologically entangled in it. In some cases, the secondary person is still reality-based but exhausted; in others, they are already drifting toward partial adoption of the belief and need closer monitoring.

Protecting the unaffected person may require practical steps that look ordinary on the surface but are clinically significant. These can include ensuring access to independent transportation, a private phone, secure documents, separate finances where possible, and a way to contact help without alerting the other person. If the relationship is controlling, these supports are not luxuries; they are part of preserving autonomy. The person may need help thinking through what to say, when to disengage, and how to respond if the delusional person becomes angry or accusatory. In high-conflict situations, even small choices—such as where to sleep, who can attend appointments, or how to leave the home safely—may carry major consequences. A realistic plan should account for those details rather than assuming the person can simply "set boundaries" in a vacuum.

At the same time, clinicians should be careful not to cast the unaffected person as fully separate from the relational system. They may feel torn between loyalty and safety, empathy and self-protection, hope and resignation. Some have participated in minimizing the problem because doing so seemed to reduce conflict. Others have been pressured into silence by fear of abandonment, retaliation, or family blame. This is why support has to be emotionally informed, not merely instructive. The person may need validation that their ambivalence makes sense, and that leaving, limiting contact, or insisting on treatment can all feel painful without being wrong. In families where the belief has become organized around caregiving, the unaffected person may also need help distinguishing compassion from overfunctioning, especially if they have taken on the role of manager, translator, or buffer for too long.

The broader family system often needs intervention even when only one or two people appear directly affected. Shared psychotic disorder tends to thrive in environments where roles become rigid and communication narrows. Other family members may have adapted by avoiding certain topics, reinforcing the dominant person's certainty, or treating the delusion as an unspoken house rule. Some may be openly skeptical but feel powerless to intervene; others may be exhausted from repeated crises and have learned that silence is easier than confrontation. In either case, the family system can unintentionally stabilize the problem by rewarding avoidance and discouraging independent reality testing. Helping the family means identifying these patterns without assigning blame. The point is to show how each person's coping style may be understandable while still sustaining the larger difficulty.

Family meetings, when appropriate, can be useful if they are structured around safety, communication, and roles rather than debate over the delusional content. The clinician may need to redirect the conversation away from proving or disproving the belief and toward questions such as who is responsible for what, how conflict is managed, and what boundaries are needed to keep everyone safe. For some families, this is the first time they have been asked to speak in terms of function rather than certainty. It can also be the first time the unaffected person hears that they are allowed to seek support without betraying the family. In households shaped by secrecy or intense loyalty, that permission can be as important as any specific behavioral plan.

Attention to the unaffected person and the family system is especially important when children, older adults, or dependent relatives are present. Even if they are not the primary focus of the shared belief, they may be absorbing fear, confusion, or distorted expectations about how reality works in the household. In such settings, the clinician has to think beyond the dyad and ask who else is being pulled into the pattern, who has the least power to resist it, and what supports are needed to keep the whole system from becoming more closed. Shared psychotic disorder is often sustained by relationship rather than by isolated conviction, and that means recovery frequently begins when someone inside the system is helped to see that the relationship itself can be changed.

CHAPTER 9

Chapter 9: Recovery, Relapse Prevention, and Long-Term Management

Recovery from shared psychotic disorder is usually less like a single event than a gradual reorganization of belief, attachment, and daily life. As the shared framework loosens, people often move through uneven periods of clarity, doubt, defensiveness, and cautious reflection before any lasting stability takes shape. That unevenness is not a sign of failure; it is part of what makes recovery clinically complex, especially when the relationship itself has been a source of safety, identity, or direction. The work that follows therefore shifts attention from acute disruption to the conditions that help change endure: recognizing how recovery unfolds, noticing when old patterns begin to reassert themselves, and supporting the slower task of building a life that is no longer organized around the delusion.

Stages of recovery and realistic expectations

Recovery from shared psychotic disorder is usually uneven at first. The earliest change is often not a complete disappearance of the delusion, but a loosening of certainty. A person may begin to question details, hesitate before repeating the belief, or notice that the emotional intensity around it is fading. That shift can be subtle enough to miss if one expects recovery to look like an abrupt breakthrough. In practice, the process often begins with small signs of distance: less urgency, fewer confrontations, more tolerance for ambiguity, and occasional moments in which the person can consider an alternate explanation without immediately rejecting it.

At this stage, it is important to expect fluctuation rather than linear progress. A person may sound more reflective one day and then return to rigid conviction the next, especially if contact with the reinforcing relationship remains strong or if stress increases. This does not necessarily mean treatment has failed. The mind rarely reorganizes a deeply embedded belief system in a straight line, and the relational habits that supported the delusion may take longer to change than the belief itself. For clinicians and families, the task is to watch the direction of movement over time, not to judge recovery by a single conversation.

The next phase usually involves a widening of perspective. The person begins to interact more with outside reality, whether through therapy, family support, separation from the reinforcing figure, or renewed contact with ordinary routines and relationships. As that happens, the delusion may lose some of its certainty simply because it is no longer being protected by constant repetition. This can be experienced as relief, grief, shame, or confusion. Some people feel embarrassed by what they previously believed; others are defensive or frightened by the possibility that they were misled. Both reactions are common. Recovery does not require immediate insight or perfect agreement about what happened. It requires enough stability for the person to tolerate a broader view of events without collapsing back into the shared system.

It is also realistic to expect that insight may arrive in pieces. A person may acknowledge that the situation became exaggerated while still holding onto some part of the original belief. Or they may recognize the relationship was controlling without yet being able to name the belief as false. That partial insight is clinically meaningful. It often marks the beginning of a more durable recovery because it creates room for reflection. In some cases, the secondary person improves first once the relational pressure is reduced, while the primary person continues to need treatment for a separate psychotic or mood disorder. In other cases, both people require ongoing intervention because the shared belief has become tied to broader psychiatric symptoms, trauma, or longstanding dependency [1][2].

Another realistic expectation is that emotional recovery lags behind cognitive recovery. Even when a person can admit that the belief was not reliable, they may still feel afraid, ashamed, or deeply attached to the person who reinforced it. The relationship itself may have served as a source of identity, safety, or purpose. When that structure weakens, the person can feel unmoored. This is one reason recovery plans often need to address more than symptom reduction. Rebuilding daily routines, restoring contact with supportive people, and helping the person develop a sense of self that is not organized around the delusion are all part of the work. Without that broader rebuilding, the old belief can remain emotionally available as a familiar refuge.

Relapse risk is highest when the original conditions return unchanged. If isolation, coercion, or intense dependency remain in place, the shared belief may reassert itself during periods of stress, conflict, or loneliness. For that reason, recovery should be understood as a process of reducing vulnerability, not merely suppressing symptoms. A person may appear well in a structured setting and then deteriorate when they return to the same closed environment that sustained the delusion. This is especially important in family systems or caregiving relationships where the social world around the person has not changed enough to support a different reality. In those settings, even genuine progress can be fragile if boundaries, supervision, and outside contact are not maintained [8][9].

There are also situations in which recovery is partial rather than complete. A person may no longer share the original delusion but remain prone to suspiciousness, dependency, or later episodes of distorted belief under stress. Others may recover from the shared aspect yet continue to struggle with depression, trauma symptoms, or a primary psychotic disorder that needs separate treatment. That is why realistic expectations matter so much. The goal is not always to return the person to exactly the same emotional and relational arrangement that existed before the illness. In many cases, the healthier outcome is a more independent life, more reliable reality testing, and a relationship structure that no longer rewards fixed false beliefs. Even when improvement is substantial, ongoing follow-up is often needed because the pattern can reappear in altered form if the underlying vulnerabilities are not addressed [7][4].

Relapse prevention planning and early warning signs

Relapse prevention in shared psychotic disorder begins with recognizing that a return of symptoms is often relational before it is fully verbal. The belief may not reappear in exactly the same form, but the conditions that once made it persuasive can return with surprising speed: renewed isolation, increased contact with the dominant person, conflict with outsiders, sleep disruption, escalating stress, or a fresh crisis that narrows attention. For that reason, a relapse plan should focus not only on the content of the delusion, but on the pattern of life around it. The most useful plans identify what changes first, what tends to follow, and which environmental pressures make the shared framework easier to rebuild.

Early warning signs are often subtle enough to be mistaken for ordinary anxiety or renewed closeness. A person may begin asking the same questions repeatedly, returning to the same explanation after brief moments of doubt, or seeking reassurance from the same source while dismissing everyone else. The language may become more absolute again: "I know," "It is happening again," "No one else understands," or "We should not talk to anyone about this." In the secondary person, early warning signs can include a quick reattachment to the primary person's certainty, a renewed reluctance to compare notes with others, or a noticeable shift from independent judgment back toward deference. Clinically, the concern is not just that the belief has returned, but that the relationship has started to function again as the main filter for reality [1] [9].

Behavioral changes often provide the clearest clues. People may resume checking, monitoring, avoiding, documenting, or confronting in ways that seem driven by urgency rather than reflection. They may stop sleeping well, stop eating regularly, or begin reorganizing routines around the belief. Social withdrawal is especially important, because relapse often thrives when the person becomes less reachable by ordinary feedback. If the pair begins limiting contact with friends, clinicians, employers, or relatives, or if one person starts speaking for both of them again, the system may be tightening in the same way it did before. In family settings, a return to secrecy, shared vigilance, or coordinated suspicion can signal that the delusional framework is being reassembled [8][9].

A practical relapse plan should identify the specific triggers that have mattered in the past. For some people, the trigger is a period of intense stress or grief. For others, it is a breakup, a move, a medical illness, financial instability, or renewed dependence on the same person who previously reinforced the belief. The plan should also note protective factors that weaken relapse: regular sleep, consistent medication when indicated for comorbid conditions, contact with noninvolved supports, and structured time away from the reinforcing relationship. Because the condition is often maintained by isolation and emotional enmeshment, prevention usually depends on widening the person's world before the belief narrows it again [6][2].

It is also important to decide in advance what to do when warning signs appear. A relapse plan is more effective when it names concrete steps rather than vague intentions. Those steps may include contacting a clinician, increasing appointment frequency, involving a trusted family member or case manager, reducing unsupervised time between the two people if that contact has historically intensified symptoms, or arranging a medical and psychiatric reassessment if there are new safety concerns. If the person has a history of self-harm, refusal of care, aggression, or dangerous attempts to act on the belief, the plan should specify when emergency services are appropriate. In one case of delusional infestation with folie à deux, suicidal ideation emerged alongside worsening symptoms, underscoring how quickly risk can rise when the belief becomes emotionally unbearable [7].

For clinicians, relapse prevention also means tracking insight over time. A person does not need to reject a belief completely for the situation to improve, but they do need enough distance to notice when certainty is hardening again. Questions such as whether the person is sleeping, whether they are less able to tolerate disagreement, whether they are avoiding outside contact, and whether the relationship is becoming more controlling can reveal a great deal before a full relapse is obvious. In some cases, the secondary person may be the first to show return of symptoms, especially if the primary person's conviction is still active. In other cases, the secondary person may begin to oscillate between doubt and compliance, which can be an early indication that the shared system is regaining strength [2][4].

Families and caregivers often need explicit guidance about what to watch for because they may mistake early relapse for stress, stubbornness, or a temporary bad mood. It helps to agree on a short list of changes that matter most: renewed secrecy, repeated checking, increased fearfulness, avoidance of ordinary activities, sudden distrust of neutral people, or a return to the same explanations that previously dominated the relationship. When these signs appear, the goal is not to argue the person back into insight. The goal is to lower arousal, reduce reinforcement, and reconnect the person to support before the belief becomes the organizing center again. Shared psychotic disorder tends to deepen when the relationship becomes more closed and more certain; relapse prevention works best when the opposite is true.

Rebuilding identity, autonomy, and healthy relationships

Recovery is not only about reducing the grip of the shared belief; it is also about restoring a person's sense of self outside the relationship that helped organize that belief. In many cases, identity has been compressed for so long that the person no longer knows where personal preference ends and relational adaptation begins. They may have learned to scan the other person's mood before naming their own, to defer in order to keep peace, or to treat closeness as proof of safety. When the shared delusion weakens, that same person can feel disoriented rather than immediately relieved. The loss of a fixed framework may expose uncertainty, grief, and a long-neglected question: Who am I when I am not protecting, echoing, or orbiting this belief?

That question matters clinically because identity repair does not happen automatically when the delusion recedes. A person may still carry the habits that made the shared system possible: chronic self-doubt, over-compliance, fear of disagreement, and a tendency to outsource judgment. If those habits remain untouched, the person can become vulnerable to replacing one organizing force with another, whether that is a different relationship, a new authority figure, or a fresh but equally rigid explanation for distress. Rebuilding identity therefore involves more than reassurance. It requires repeated opportunities to make small, independent decisions and to experience those decisions as legitimate. The process often begins with ordinary choices—what to eat, whom to call, how to spend an hour alone—but these choices matter because they reintroduce agency in concrete form.

Autonomy grows best when it is treated as a skill rather than a personality trait. Some people emerge from a shared psychotic system with little practice in tolerating disagreement or uncertainty. They may feel anxious when they are not being guided, or guilty when they act without checking with the other person. Clinically, it can help to frame independence as a gradual strengthening of internal reference points: noticing one's own thoughts, comparing them with external information, and allowing doubt without collapsing into panic. This is especially important after periods of isolation or coercive influence, when the person may have been conditioned to treat private judgment as dangerous. A measured return to autonomy often includes predictable routines, clear boundaries, and support that encourages reflection rather than dependency.

Healthy relationships after recovery need a different structure from the one that sustained the delusion. The goal is not simply to reconnect, but to build connections that do not require surrendering reality testing or personal boundaries. That means encouraging relationships in which disagreement is safe, privacy is respected, and affection is not contingent on agreement. For some people, this will involve repairing family ties that became strained during the illness. For others, it will mean creating distance from a person who continued to reinforce distorted beliefs or who used emotional dependence to maintain control. In either case, the standard is the same: a relationship should make it easier, not harder, to think clearly, ask questions, and remain grounded in shared reality.

This work can be complicated by shame. After the delusion loosens, the person may look back on their behavior with embarrassment or self-reproach, especially if others were harmed, frightened, or excluded. Shame can make recovery feel socially risky, and it may tempt the person to withdraw or to avoid new relationships altogether. That reaction is understandable, but prolonged withdrawal can recreate the very conditions that made the shared belief persuasive in the first place. A more useful approach is to separate accountability from self-condemnation. The person may need to acknowledge what happened, repair what can be repaired, and learn from the experience without turning that experience into a permanent identity. Recovery is helped by relationships that can hold complexity: care without denial, honesty without humiliation, and limits without abandonment.

For clinicians and caregivers, the practical task is to support connection while resisting overprotection. It is easy, after a frightening episode, to treat the person as fragile in a way that quietly undermines their agency. Yet autonomy cannot be rebuilt if every decision is managed on their behalf. The more durable approach is collaborative: asking what feels manageable, identifying situations that still trigger fear or dependence, and helping the person rehearse responses that preserve dignity and choice. In cases where the relationship itself was the main carrier of the delusion, recovery may also require learning how to relate without enmeshment—how to stay connected without merging, how to care without controlling, and how to disagree without interpreting disagreement as abandonment. Those relational capacities are often the true markers of long-term healing [1][9][4].

Long-term follow-up, support networks, and community resources

Long-term follow-up matters because shared psychotic disorder does not always resolve when the most obvious crisis has passed. Even when the delusional system loosens, the people involved may remain vulnerable to the same conditions that allowed it to form: isolation, emotional dependence, unresolved trauma, family conflict, or a relationship structure in which one person's certainty still carries unusual weight. Follow-up care therefore has to look beyond symptom reduction and ask whether the person's daily life is becoming more independent, more reality-based, and more connected to sources of feedback outside the original dyad. In practice, that often means continuing contact after the acute episode has settled, especially when the relationship itself was central to the problem.

For clinicians, the follow-up period is an opportunity to watch for subtle shifts rather than waiting for full relapse. A person may not return to the exact same belief, but may begin showing the same pattern of narrowing: fewer outside contacts, renewed deference to the dominant person, increased preoccupation with a suspicious explanation, or growing resistance to disagreement. These changes can appear gradually and may be easier to detect in routine check-ins than in crisis appointments. When the original presentation included medical concerns, such as infestation beliefs, the person may also drift back into repeated self-examination, reassurance seeking, or avoidance of ordinary care, even if they no longer speak about the delusion in the same terms [5][7].

Follow-up is also where treatment gains are either consolidated or lost. If the secondary person has begun to separate from the shared belief, that progress can be fragile. A return to the same living arrangement, the same conversational patterns, or the same emotional hierarchy may quickly reactivate the old framework. For that reason, long-term planning often includes practical steps that are easy to underestimate: keeping sleep stable, preserving appointments, maintaining contact with at least one grounded support person, and reducing prolonged periods of isolation. In some cases, the most important question is not whether the belief is gone today, but whether the person has enough distance from the original relational pressure to notice if it begins to return.

Support networks play a protective role precisely because shared psychotic disorder tends to thrive where perspective is limited. A broad network does not have to be large to be useful. One steady friend, a relative who can remain calm, a therapist, a primary care clinician, a case manager, or a support group can each provide a small but meaningful corrective to the closed logic of the delusional system. The value of these relationships is not that they argue the person out of the belief. Their value is that they widen the field of reality, making it harder for one relationship to define everything. When the person affected has spent years relying on a single attachment figure, rebuilding a wider social map may be as important as any direct symptom intervention.

For families, support networks often need to be structured rather than improvised. It is easy for relatives to drift into two unhelpful extremes: either they become overly cautious and avoid all discussion, or they become exhausted and try to force change through repeated confrontation. A healthier network has clear roles. One person may help with transportation, another with appointments, another with practical problem-solving, while all of them agree not to reinforce the delusion. This kind of coordination reduces the chance that the family will be split into allies and opponents, a split that can intensify the shared system. It also protects the unaffected person, who may otherwise become the default container for everyone else's fear, frustration, or disbelief.

Community resources become especially important when the relationship has been isolated from ordinary supports or when the person needs more than informal family help can provide. Outpatient psychotherapy, psychiatric follow-up, community mental health centers, peer support programs, case management services, domestic violence resources, and crisis lines can all serve different functions depending on the situation. Some people need help with housing, transportation, or benefits before they can fully engage in therapy. Others need a setting where they can speak privately and consistently without the dominant person present. In more complex cases, community clinicians can also help coordinate between mental health care and primary care, which is important when physical complaints, medication side effects, or substance use are part of the picture [1][4].

The best use of community resources is often preventive rather than reactive. A person who has recovered from a shared delusion may still benefit from periodic check-ins, especially during major stressors such as bereavement, financial strain, illness, or relationship change. Likewise, families may need a standing plan for what to do if suspiciousness, fear, or dependency starts to intensify again. That plan works best when it names concrete contacts, preferred clinics, emergency options, and the point at which the situation has crossed from concern into urgent risk. Shared psychotic disorder is rare, but the relational vulnerabilities around it are not. Long-term support is what helps keep a temporary recovery from becoming another closed system.

CHAPTER 10

Chapter 10: Ethical, Cultural, and Legal Considerations

Before the clinical picture can be translated into action, it has to pass through a set of responsibilities that are easy to overlook when attention is fixed on symptoms alone. Shared psychotic disorder often places clinicians, families, and caregivers in situations where ordinary boundaries are strained by urgency, trust, fear, and unequal power. In those moments, the central task is not simply to identify the belief, but to respond in ways that are careful, proportionate, and respectful of the people involved. That requires attention to the limits of one's role, to the social meanings attached to the presentation, and to the potential consequences of every decision about disclosure, participation, and intervention.

Ethical responsibilities in high-risk or coercive situations

Ethical responsibility becomes most visible when the situation is no longer just clinically puzzling but potentially dangerous. In shared psychotic disorder, the delusional system may be bound up with threats of self-harm, refusal of food or medication, attempts to confront an imagined persecutor, or escalating control by one person over another. At that point, the clinician's obligation is not to remain neutral in the abstract sense, but to act in a way that protects life, preserves dignity, and does not deepen the coercive structure already present in the relationship. Ethical practice requires attention to both the content of the belief and the social conditions surrounding it, because a false belief can be harmful in one context and immediately hazardous in another.

One of the most important duties is to recognize when apparent "consent" is not truly free. A secondary person may agree to treatment, refuse help, or repeat the shared belief while under intense emotional pressure, fear of abandonment, dependence on the primary person, or direct intimidation. In those cases, the clinician should not assume that verbal agreement reflects autonomous choice. It may be necessary to speak with each person separately, assess whether the person can disagree safely, and look for signs that the relationship itself is functioning as a source of compulsion. This matters especially when the more dominant person controls access to transportation, money, communication, medication, housing, or information. Shared psychotic disorder can be reinforced by exactly these forms of control, and the ethical response must address the power imbalance rather than treating the pair as if both parties occupy equal ground.

Confidentiality also becomes more complicated in high-risk or coercive situations. Families often want full disclosure, and the people involved may present as a unit, but ethical care does not allow the clinician to collapse one person's privacy into the other's needs. Information should be shared only to the extent permitted by law, consent, and safety requirements. At the same time, rigid secrecy can be harmful if it prevents coordination around imminent risk. The clinician has to distinguish between ordinary family involvement, which may support care, and family participation that would expose one person to retaliation or further manipulation. When the relationship is coercive, even well-meaning disclosure can become a tool of control if it is not handled carefully.

In practice, this means documenting concerns with precision and restraint. Records should describe observed behavior, reported beliefs, relational dynamics, and specific risk indicators rather than adopting the delusional framework as if it were fact. Careful documentation protects continuity of care and helps justify protective action if the situation deteriorates. It also guards against a common ethical failure: minimizing the danger because the belief sounds bizarre or because the relationship has long been normalized by those inside it. A delusion involving poisoning, stalking, infestation, spiritual attack, or surveillance may prompt dangerous actions even when no external threat exists. The ethical issue is not whether the belief is understandable; it is whether it is driving unsafe decisions or preventing needed care.

When coercion is present, the clinician may need to shift from a purely therapeutic stance to a protective one. That can include recommending a higher level of care, involving psychiatry urgently, consulting social work, or, when legally indicated, initiating emergency evaluation. In some cases, the least harmful option is temporary separation, because the shared belief is being maintained through constant contact, surveillance, or reinforcement. Separation should never be treated casually, since it can provoke distress or retaliation, but neither should it be avoided simply because it is uncomfortable. If the relationship is preventing reality testing, blocking treatment, or exposing someone to abuse, the ethical duty to reduce harm may outweigh the preference to preserve the status quo.

There is also an ethical obligation to avoid colluding with the dominant person's version of events. A clinician who overidentifies with the more articulate or authoritative party can inadvertently reinforce the same hierarchy that sustains the delusion. This risk is especially high when the primary person is persuasive, distressed, or presents as the "reasonable" one while the secondary person appears confused or passive. Ethical practice requires deliberate curiosity about whose account has been centered, whose fear has been normalized, and whose independence may be shrinking. In coercive situations, neutrality can become a form of inaction if it allows the more powerful person to keep defining reality for everyone else.

The same principle applies to families and caregivers who are trying to help. They may feel pressure to choose between confrontation and silence, but ethical support usually lies in a narrower middle path: neither validating the delusion nor escalating the conflict, while remaining attentive to danger, abuse, and loss of autonomy. When a person is being isolated, monitored, threatened, or prevented from obtaining care, the ethical response is not only emotional support but active protection. Shared psychotic disorder is unusual, but the responsibilities it creates are familiar at their core: assess power honestly, protect the vulnerable, and refuse to let closeness obscure harm.

Cultural competence and avoiding misdiagnosis

Cultural context can change the meaning of beliefs, behaviors, and relationships in ways that are easy to miss if the clinician assumes that one cultural framework fits all patients. What looks suspicious, bizarre, or overly dependent in one setting may be ordinary, morally neutral, or even expected in another. Strong family loyalty, deference to elders, spiritual interpretation of suffering, or reliance on a trusted authority figure may be normative features of a person's cultural world rather than signs of psychopathology. In shared psychotic disorder, this matters because the clinical picture is already shaped by closeness, trust, and limited outside feedback. If those same features are also culturally reinforced, the boundary between culturally patterned belief and delusional fixation becomes harder to draw.

A careful assessment therefore begins with curiosity rather than assumption. The clinician has to ask what the belief means to the person, how it is understood within the family or community, and whether it is shared widely enough to be considered culturally sanctioned. A belief that seems unusual from the outside may still fall within a religious, spiritual, or cultural tradition that gives it coherent meaning. At the same time, cultural explanation does not rule out a psychotic process. The key question is not simply whether a belief is uncommon, but whether it is fixed in the face of contrary evidence, causing impairment, narrowing functioning, or drawing others into a shared reality that becomes increasingly resistant to reflection. The cultural formulation is not an alternative to diagnosis; it is part of how diagnosis becomes accurate.

Misdiagnosis often occurs in both directions. On one side, clinicians may pathologize beliefs or practices they do not understand, especially when those beliefs are expressed in unfamiliar language, through indirect communication, or in a style that differs from mainstream clinical norms.

On the other side, they may miss a developing shared delusion because they interpret it as a culturally acceptable worldview, a family-specific habit, or a response to stress that does not seem "psychotic enough" to raise concern. Either error can be costly. Overpathologizing can damage trust, stigmatize a family, or lead to unnecessary coercive intervention. Under-recognizing the disorder can allow the belief system to deepen, prolong distress, and delay treatment until the situation has become much more entrenched.

Language and interpretation deserve special attention. A patient who speaks through an interpreter may sound more circumstantial, guarded, or emotionally intense than they would in their first language, and that can distort the clinician's impression of thought process or conviction. Cultural idioms of distress may also present as physical complaints, moral language, or spiritual descriptions rather than explicit psychiatric symptoms. In some communities, talking about persecution, hexing, spirits, curses, or supernatural harm may be a culturally recognized way to describe suffering. The clinician's task is not to dismiss these expressions, but to determine whether they are shared explanatory frameworks or whether they have become rigid, self-sealing beliefs that are driving behavior in ways that are clinically significant.

Shared psychotic disorder is especially vulnerable to misdiagnosis when the relationship itself is viewed without cultural context. In some families, strong interdependence is expected and even valued; in some caregiving systems, one person's authority is rarely questioned; in some communities, collective decision-making is the norm. These patterns can resemble the enmeshment or dominance seen in shared delusional systems, but they are not automatically pathological. The distinction lies in flexibility, reciprocity, and reality testing. Culturally shaped closeness usually leaves room for disagreement, outside input, and adjustment. A shared psychotic process tends to narrow that room. The pair or family becomes less able to tolerate alternative explanations, and dissent begins to feel dangerous, disloyal, or impossible.

Clinicians reduce the risk of misdiagnosis by asking practical, culturally informed questions: Who else in the patient's community holds this belief? How is it usually discussed? What would a trusted elder, faith leader, or family member say about it? Has the belief changed the person's functioning, sleep, safety, or willingness to accept help? These questions do not replace diagnostic judgment, but they help separate cultural meaning from psychopathology. They also reveal whether the belief is embedded in a broader social framework or has become unusually private, intense, and insulating. A belief that is culturally shared can still be clinically relevant if it is escalating into fear, impairment, or coercive control, but the clinician should understand the social context before naming it as delusional.

Respectful consultation can be helpful when uncertainty remains. Involving cultural brokers, interpreters, or clinicians familiar with the patient's background can prevent premature conclusions and reduce the chance that the assessment becomes centered on the clinician's discomfort rather than the patient's experience. That approach is especially important in cases where race, migration history, religion, poverty, or social marginalization may shape how the patient has been treated by institutions in the past. People who have been misunderstood before are often quick to recognize when a clinician is relying on stereotypes instead of careful listening. Cultural competence, in this setting, is not an abstract professional ideal; it is part of building enough trust to see the difference between a belief that reflects a shared worldview and one that reflects a shared delusion [6].

Confidentiality, consent, and family involvement

Confidentiality in shared psychotic disorder is rarely simple, because the clinical picture often involves more than one person whose accounts, fears, and loyalties are tightly linked. A clinician may be meeting separately with the primary and secondary person, or with a family system in which several members have been drawn into the same belief structure. In either case, the ordinary promise of privacy has to be balanced against the reality that information shared by one person may affect the safety, treatment, and trust of others. The first responsibility is to be explicit about the limits of confidentiality from the beginning: what can remain private, what may need to be shared for treatment coordination, and under what circumstances information must be disclosed to protect safety. When those boundaries are vague, family members may assume that the clinician will relay everything, while the patient may assume that nothing will be shared. Both assumptions can damage treatment.

Consent is equally important, but it is not always straightforward when insight is limited or when one person appears to speak for the other. Each adult should be approached as an individual patient whenever possible, with separate attention to capacity, willingness, and understanding. Consent is meaningful only when the person can grasp the nature of the evaluation or intervention, the likely benefits and risks, and the practical consequences of refusing care. In a shared delusional system, that understanding may be partially compromised by fear, coercion, dependency, or confusion. The clinician should not assume that agreement expressed in the presence of a dominant relative reflects free choice. It may be necessary to speak privately, repeat explanations in plain language, and confirm understanding more than once. If a person cannot give informed consent for a specific intervention, the clinician must follow the applicable legal and ethical standards for substitute decision-making, emergency treatment, or protective action.

Family involvement can be therapeutic, but only when it is structured carefully. The presence of relatives, partners, or caregivers may provide crucial collateral information, help with monitoring risk, and strengthen the person's connection to care. At the same time, family participation can also intensify conflict or reinforce the delusion if everyone is pulled into arguing about its content. It is usually more useful to focus family discussions on observable behavior, distress, and safety than on proving whether the belief is true. A relative can report that the person is sleeping poorly, refusing meals, checking the home repeatedly, or becoming increasingly isolated without being asked to endorse or refute the delusion. This keeps the conversation anchored in clinical reality rather than in a contest over certainty.

There are also situations in which involving family too broadly can be harmful. If one person is the source of coercion, surveillance, or emotional dominance, then inviting that person into every conversation may silence the more vulnerable individual and strengthen the existing power imbalance. In those cases, the clinician may need to separate contacts, limit what is discussed in joint sessions, or schedule individual meetings to preserve a space where the less dominant person can speak freely. This is especially important when a caregiver or partner controls transportation, medication, finances, or access to outside support. A person who appears "agreeable" in front of the dominant family member may give a very different account when interviewed alone.

Documentation should be careful and restrained. The record needs enough detail to support continuity of care, risk assessment, and future decision-making, but it should not turn into a repository of speculative labels or emotionally loaded interpretations. It is better to document specific statements, observed behaviors, reported concerns, and the rationale for any disclosure than to record only conclusions about who is "delusional" or who is "the inducer." In complex family situations, precise documentation can be especially important if later treatment teams need to understand why confidentiality was limited, why a particular relative was included or excluded, or why an emergency intervention was considered necessary. The goal is to make the clinical reasoning transparent without unnecessarily inflaming the family system.

Clinicians should also explain that confidentiality does not mean isolation from care. Patients and families sometimes hear privacy as a barrier, when in fact it is meant to support honest communication. A person is more likely to disclose fear, shame, or ambivalence if they know the clinician will not automatically relay every detail to other relatives. At the same time, the clinician can clarify that if there is imminent risk of harm, abuse, neglect, or inability to care for basic needs, privacy may have to give way to protective action. That distinction helps reduce the false choice between total secrecy and total exposure. It also makes it easier to ask for consent to involve specific people for specific purposes, rather than treating family involvement as all-or-nothing.

In practice, the most careful approach is often a staged one: meet privately first, clarify consent and limits, gather collateral information where appropriate, and then invite family participation only to the extent that it serves treatment and safety. When handled well, confidentiality protects dignity, consent protects autonomy, and family involvement provides support without surrendering clinical judgment to the dynamics of the shared belief. In a condition defined by blurred boundaries between minds, those distinctions matter all the more.

Legal issues, protective interventions, and documentation

Legal concerns arise in shared psychotic disorder when unusual beliefs begin to affect consent, safety, autonomy, or the ability to function in ordinary life. The condition itself is not a legal category, but the behaviors surrounding it can trigger legal scrutiny in several settings: emergency evaluation, involuntary treatment, child or elder protection, guardianship disputes, housing instability, workplace conflict, and family court matters. The law is generally less interested in the label than in the practical question of whether a person can make informed decisions and whether anyone is at imminent risk of harm. That distinction matters, because a shared delusion may be clinically significant long before it becomes legally actionable, yet once danger escalates, clinicians and caregivers may need to respond quickly and within the limits of local law.

Capacity is often the first legal issue to consider. A person may be able to discuss everyday matters clearly while still being unable to weigh information realistically when the delusion touches treatment, finances, or personal safety. If a belief is driving refusal of essential medical care, unsafe travel, abandonment of housing, or confrontation with an imagined threat, the question becomes whether the person can understand the situation, appreciate consequences, reason about options, and communicate a choice. In shared psychotic disorder, capacity may be complicated by the influence of another person who reinforces the delusion, especially when the relationship itself is coercive or highly dependent. Clinicians should avoid assuming that agreement between two people equals valid consent; two people can reinforce one another while both remain impaired in judgment.

Protective interventions are usually justified by risk, not by disagreement with a belief. When there is imminent danger of self-harm, violence, severe neglect, inability to care for basic needs, or exposure to exploitation, the response may need to move beyond outpatient support. That can mean emergency psychiatric evaluation, a welfare check, temporary separation from the reinforcing relationship, or, in some circumstances, involuntary assessment or hospitalization under applicable law. The goal is not punishment or forced correction of belief. It is reduction of immediate harm and restoration of enough stability for thoughtful evaluation to occur. In cases involving children, dependent adults, or older adults, mandatory reporting obligations may also apply if the shared delusion is contributing to neglect, abuse, or unsafe supervision.

Restrictive interventions should be matched to the level of risk and used with careful attention to proportionality. A protective plan may include involving crisis services, coordinating with primary care or psychiatry, arranging supervised contact, limiting access to weapons or other means of harm, or helping a vulnerable person leave an unsafe environment. In some families, the most effective intervention is not a dramatic legal action but a structured separation from the person most strongly reinforcing the delusion, combined with practical support for housing, transportation, communication, and follow-up care. When coercion, intimidation, or financial control are present, legal remedies such as protective orders, emergency custody arrangements, or adult protective services may become relevant, depending on jurisdiction and circumstances.

Documentation is essential because shared psychotic disorder often involves multiple accounts, shifting alliances, and rapid changes in presentation. Good documentation should describe observable behavior, direct quotations when possible, the sequence of events, collateral information, and the specific reasons for concern. It is better to record that a person stated, "My neighbor is sending poison through the vents," than to summarize vaguely that the person was "paranoid." Likewise, if a caregiver reports that the person has not eaten for two days because of fear of contamination, that detail should be documented as a concrete risk factor. Clear notes help other professionals understand the clinical picture, support continuity of care, and show why a particular intervention was chosen.

Documentation should also distinguish facts from inference. The record can note that a person refused medication after consulting with a partner who strongly endorsed the delusion, but it should not overstate motive unless the person's own words or behavior support that interpretation. When there is uncertainty, the chart should reflect it. That includes noting collateral sources, the presence or absence of insight, the results of safety assessment, and any attempts to engage the person in voluntary care before more restrictive measures were considered. In legal settings, this level of specificity is often what makes the difference between a clinically useful record and one that appears speculative or biased.

Because shared psychotic disorder can involve more than one affected person, documentation should be careful about privacy boundaries. Information from one person should be recorded and shared according to consent rules, confidentiality requirements, and any applicable duty to protect or report. When separate interviews are conducted, the clinician should note what was said in each setting and avoid blending accounts in a way that obscures whose perspective is being reported. If a decision is made to involve law enforcement, emergency services, or child and adult protective systems, the rationale should be explicit: what was observed, what risk was identified, what alternatives were considered, and why the chosen step was necessary. In a condition where reality testing may be fragile and relationships may be controlling, precise documentation is not merely administrative. It is part of the protective response itself.

Citations

The following sources were referenced in the preceding chapters. Each entry links back to the inline reference in the text. All sources were verified against the OpenAlex academic database at the time of generation.

1. Danilo Arnone, Anish Patel, Giles Ming-Yee Tan (2006). The nosological significance of Folie à Deux: a review of the literature. https://doi.org/10.1186/1744-859x-5-11

2. Sanja Bjelan, Milana Okanovic, Ana-Marija Vejnović et al. (2022). Folie à deux - a case report. https://doi.org/10.2298/mpn-s2204123b

3. S. Castelao-Almodóvar, Anna Riva, Raquel Perez et al. (2025). Shared psychosis at a distance: a case of telephone-induced Folie à Deux. https://doi.org/10.1192/j.eurpsy.2025.2208

4. E. Arroyo Sánchez, P. Setién Preciados, C. Díaz Mayoral (2024). “Folie à deux,” or shared psychosis: A case report. https://doi.org/10.1192/j.eurpsy.2024.1555

5. Adam Reich, Dominika Kwiatkowska, Przemysław Pacan (2019). Delusions of Parasitosis: An Update. https://doi.org/10.1007/s13555-019-00324-3

6. Pierfrancesco Maria Balducci, Chiara Gobbicchi, Patrizia Moretti et al. (2017). Delusional sharing: a history focus-on and case report of folie à deux. https://doi.org/10.1708/2737.27910

7. Christina Kalovidouri, Łukasz Kowalewski, Dragos Virgil Mos et al. (2022). A Case of Delusional Parasitosis With Folie à Deux Treated With Low-Dose Quetiapine. https://doi.org/10.7759/cureus.25344

8. Gökçe Işıl Kurmuş, Hanife Karataş, Elif Erdem et al. (2025). Shared Delusional Parasitosis in Two Families: Clinical Insights Into Folie à Deux and Folie à Trois. https://doi.org/10.2196/78398

9. Christian Galindo, Lesmer Galindo (2025). Folie à Deux in the Family Environment: A Case of Shared Delusion Between a Mother and Her Son. https://doi.org/10.7759/cureus.78703

10. Vindyanita Simanjuntak (2026). When Delusions Become Shared: A Study of Folie À Deux in the Context of Paranoid Schizophrenia and Cultural Values. https://doi.org/10.58344/locus.v5i5.5806

11. Carlos A. Bernal-Rocha, Jessica Treviño-Lozano, Mónica R. Cid-Ortega et al. (2024). Folie à deux: a case of a wife and husband and a literature review. https://doi.org/10.24875/rmu.24000005

12. Tengku Mohd Saifuddin Tengku Kamarulbahri, Rosliza Yahaya (2024). Diagnostic conundrum: A rare case of psychosis in leptospirosis among siblings with folie à trois. https://doi.org/10.5505/kpd.2024.87528

13. Alexander Dimitriev, Azim Sagitov (2025). The Mirror Psychopathology Hypothesis (Sagitov–Dimitriev): A Neurobiological Model of Empathic Transmission of Mental States. https://doi.org/10.22541/au.176037787.74155743/v1

14. Gilles Martínez (2017). Autism-schizophrenia continuum : contribution of the study of social cognition and developmental phenotypic markers. https://openalex.org/W4393352073

Conclusion

When the delusional system begins to loosen, the change is often quiet before it is obvious. A person may not announce that they no longer believe the shared idea. More often, they begin to pause before repeating it, ask more questions, or show a new willingness to consider that another explanation might exist. These moments matter because they mark the return of internal distance. The belief is still present, but it no longer occupies the mind with the same total authority.

That early distance can be fragile. In shared psychotic disorder, the person who has been most influenced may still organize much of daily life around the relationship that carried the belief. If that relationship remains unchanged, the old certainty can reassert itself quickly. Recovery therefore depends not only on symptom reduction, but on whether the surrounding structure of dependence, isolation, and reinforcement has changed enough to support a different way of thinking. Without that shift, the mind may return to the most familiar explanation whenever stress rises or uncertainty becomes difficult to bear.

For this reason, long-term stability is often built in layers rather than achieved through a single turning point. First comes safety: reducing immediate danger, interrupting escalating behavior, and making sure basic needs are met. Then comes distance from the conditions that kept the belief alive, whether that means changes in living arrangements, changes in contact, or more consistent access to outside support. Only after that does deeper work become possible, including rebuilding judgment, testing reality in small ways, and restoring a sense of personal agency.

The relationship itself may also need to be redefined. In some cases, the person who served as the source of the delusional framework is still part of the secondary person's life, but the terms of contact must change. That may require firmer boundaries, supervision, separate treatment plans, or limits on conversations that repeatedly pull both people back into the same false certainty. If the relationship cannot be safely reshaped, recovery may remain partial. The clinical task is not to preserve closeness at any cost, but to determine what kind of contact can exist without reactivating the pattern.

Families and caregivers often need time to adjust to this slower pace of change. They may hope for a clear break, only to find that progress comes in uneven steps: a period of insight followed by defensiveness, a calmer week followed by renewed suspicion, a small act of independence followed by retreat. These fluctuations do not necessarily mean treatment has failed. They reflect how deeply the shared belief was woven into emotion, identity, and daily routine. Patience is important, but patience must be paired with structure. Unstructured reassurance can easily become another form of reinforcement.

One of the most important long-term goals is helping the affected person rebuild a life that is not organized around the delusion or the relationship that sustained it. That means more than stopping a false belief. It means restoring ordinary sources of stability: work, school, friendships, routines, sleep, movement, and contact with people who can offer reality-based feedback without humiliation or coercion. As those supports return, the person is less likely to depend on a single relationship for emotional certainty.

Identity is often part of this recovery in a way that is easy to overlook. A person who has spent months or years adapting to another's certainty may have lost touch with their own preferences, doubts, and boundaries. Rebuilding autonomy can therefore feel disorienting at first. It may bring grief, guilt, or fear of abandonment. Those reactions are understandable. The shift away from a shared delusional system is not only a cognitive correction; it is also a relational loss. A person may be leaving behind the very structure that once made life feel organized, however distorted that structure was.

Because of that complexity, relapse prevention has to be practical rather than abstract. The aim is to identify the conditions that reliably weaken judgment and narrow perspective. Common triggers include renewed isolation, sleep disruption, untreated anxiety or depression, escalating conflict, contact with a highly influential or controlling person, and fresh stressors that make a simple explanation feel emotionally necessary. When these conditions appear, the risk is not only that the original belief will return, but that a new version of it will emerge with the same emotional force.

Care plans are strongest when they include more than one point of support. A single therapist, family member, or physician may not be enough if the relationship dynamics remain intense. Ongoing care often benefits from coordination across mental health, primary care, social services, and, when appropriate, community supports that reduce isolation. The more distributed the support, the less likely it is that one person's certainty will dominate the entire field of experience.

It is also important to leave room for the possibility that recovery will be incomplete or uneven. Some people regain clear insight and maintain it. Others continue to have residual suspiciousness, partial conviction, or vulnerability under stress. In those cases, the goal shifts from expecting permanent resolution to maintaining enough stability that life can proceed safely and meaningfully. That may include monitoring for early warning signs, revisiting boundaries, and returning to treatment quickly if the pattern starts to tighten again.

Shared psychotic disorder can be difficult to recognize, difficult to interrupt, and difficult to live through, but it is not beyond clinical response. The condition becomes less powerful when the relationship that sustains it is no longer the only source of meaning, safety, and interpretation. Over time, the person who once borrowed another's reality can begin to recover a reality of their own—one shaped by perspective, connection, and the gradual return of trust in what can be observed, questioned, and revised.

Appendix: Practical Tools and Reference Materials

The materials that follow are meant to make the book usable at the moment when uncertainty turns practical: when a pattern needs to be noticed, a conversation needs to be started, or help needs to be found without delay. They are intentionally concise, because in situations shaped by shared delusion, clarity and brevity often matter more than explanation. Some readers will use these pages as a quiet review before a difficult meeting; others may return to them in the middle of a crisis, when memory, stress, and divided loyalties make it hard to think in sequence. The checklist, questions, glossary, and resource guide are arranged to support that kind of real-world use, offering a compact reference point that can be revisited as circumstances change. They are not a substitute for clinical judgment, but they can help organize it when the pressure is high and the next step has to be chosen carefully.

Quick-reference warning sign checklist

Use the following checklist when a relationship begins to feel organized around one person's certainty and the other person's increasing agreement. No single item proves shared psychotic disorder on its own; the concern rises when several signs appear together and persist over time.

- A fixed false belief that resists ordinary evidence and does not soften when facts, reassurance, or practical explanations are offered.
- One person appears to "carry" the belief first, and the other person later adopts the same idea, often with similar language or identical details.
- The second person becomes more confident in the belief after repeated contact with the first, especially when outside feedback is limited.
- Conversation narrows around the belief, with frequent repetition, checking, reassurance-seeking, or attempts to prove the idea to others.
- Outside perspectives are dismissed as ignorant, hostile, disloyal, or part of the imagined threat.
- The relationship becomes increasingly isolated, with fewer contacts outside the pair or family system and less willingness to hear other views.
- Daily routines begin to reorganize around the belief, including monitoring, avoidance, investigation, protective rituals, or confrontation.
- Sleep, appetite, work, school, or self-care decline because attention is consumed by the shared idea.
- Judgment becomes more rigid, with poor flexibility, impulsive decisions, or refusal to consider safer alternatives.
- Fear, suspicion, or urgency spreads through the relationship, making ordinary events feel charged with special meaning.
- The more dominant person strongly shapes interpretation by deciding what counts as evidence, what is dangerous, and what must be done.
- The less dominant person becomes increasingly dependent, deferential, or hesitant to disagree even when uncertainty is present.
- Both people begin to reinforce each other's certainty, creating a closed loop in which doubt is quickly corrected or suppressed.

• The belief causes concrete harm, such as conflict, medical refusal, financial strain, legal trouble, or breakdown in functioning.

• Attempts to discuss the belief lead to marked distress or anger, especially if the discussion threatens the relationship itself.

Several patterns deserve particular attention because they often signal that the situation is moving beyond an eccentric belief and into clinically concerning territory. A person who once seemed doubtful but now speaks with the same conviction as the more dominant partner may be showing a genuine shift in reality testing. Likewise, when two people begin using the same unusual explanation to interpret unrelated events, the shared belief may be expanding rather than remaining static. In case literature, shared delusional systems have been documented in close pairs and even in larger family constellations [8][9][2], which is one reason clinicians pay close attention to whether the belief is spreading through a relational network rather than staying confined to one individual.

Another red flag is the loss of ordinary correction. In healthy relationships, people can disagree, tolerate uncertainty, and revise a view when it no longer fits the facts. In a shared psychotic pattern, that capacity narrows. The pair may begin treating every contradiction as proof of danger, every question as betrayal, and every outsider as suspect. This closed style of thinking can be especially difficult to spot when the relationship already appears intense, loyal, or highly private. It may look like mutual support from the outside while functioning internally as a system that blocks reality-testing.

Watch for changes in behavior as much as changes in speech. The belief may be most visible in actions: repeated checking, avoidance of certain places or people, recording "evidence," discarding belongings, refusing medication, calling authorities, or making plans based on the delusion. Some cases present with distress severe enough to trigger emergency care or suicidal thinking [7], which is why the presence of self-harm, threats, or refusal of essential treatment should never be minimized. Even when the content of the belief seems unusual rather than dangerous, the behavioral consequences can still become serious quickly.

It is also important to note when the relationship itself becomes part of the symptom picture. If one person cannot think clearly without the other's approval, if disagreement consistently leads to panic or collapse, or if the bond has become a substitute for external reality, the risk rises. Shared psychotic disorder is often described in the context of close emotional bonds and isolation [1][6][4], and that relational closeness can make the warning signs easy to miss until the pattern is well established. A quick checklist cannot replace assessment, but it can help identify when a private conviction has begun to function as a shared closed system.

If several items on this list are present, especially if the belief is escalating, causing harm, or shutting out outside contact, the situation warrants professional evaluation rather than informal reassurance alone. The more the pattern depends on one person's certainty and the other person's growing compliance, the more important it becomes to look at safety, function, and the structure of the relationship, not just the content of the belief.

Suggested questions for clinical or caregiver conversations

When the clinical picture is still uncertain, the most useful questions are often the ones that slow the conversation down without forcing agreement. They should help the clinician or caregiver understand who first raised the concern, how strongly each person holds it, what the belief has changed in daily life, and whether the relationship itself is helping to maintain the conviction. In shared psychotic disorder, the aim is not to "catch" someone in a contradiction. It is to learn how the belief functions inside the relationship and whether either person can still step back from it. Questions that invite description rather than debate tend to be most informative, especially when trust is fragile or defensiveness is high.

For the person who seems to have carried the belief first, it can help to ask about the origin and development of the idea: "When did you first notice this?" "What made it feel true at the time?" "Has anything ever made you doubt it, even briefly?" "What happens when other people disagree?" These questions are useful because they reveal whether the belief has become fixed, whether it is linked to fear or stress, and whether the person can still tolerate uncertainty. A caregiver or clinician may also ask, "What do you do differently because of this belief?" or "How has it affected sleep, eating, work, or relationships?" That shifts attention from the content of the belief to its cost, which is often easier to discuss and clinically more useful than arguing about whether the belief is correct.

For the person who may have adopted the belief, the conversation often needs to be even more careful. Questions such as "When did this start making sense to you?" "What was your reaction when you first heard it?" "Did you agree right away, or did it take time?" and "Do you ever experience it differently when you are alone or away from the other person?" can clarify whether the belief was absorbed gradually through closeness and repetition. It is also helpful to ask, "What do you notice in your own body or mood when the topic comes up?" because anxiety, fear, and vigilance often reveal how much the belief has become emotionally organized rather than simply intellectually accepted. In some cases, the person may describe the belief as something they "know" only when they are with the other individual, which can be an important clue that the shared system is relationally reinforced.

Questions about the relationship itself are often the most revealing. A clinician might ask, "Who usually makes decisions?" "What happens when you disagree?" "How much time do you spend together?" "Who else knows about this?" "Has anyone outside the relationship offered another perspective?" "What tends to happen after someone questions the belief?" These questions help identify dependency, isolation, and dominance without using labels that may shut the conversation down. In family or caregiving settings, it can also be useful to ask, "Who is responsible for medication, appointments, finances, or daily routines?" and "Are there times when one person speaks for both?" Such questions can uncover whether one person's certainty has become the organizing force for the other person's reality.

When the conversation is with a caregiver or concerned family member, the wording should stay concrete and behavior-focused. Instead of asking whether the person "is delusional," it is often better to ask, "What changes have you noticed in their behavior?" "Have they become more isolated or suspicious?" "Are they avoiding work, school, food, sleep, or medical care?" "Have they started checking, documenting, confronting, or protecting themselves in unusual ways?" "What happens when you try to offer a different explanation?" A caregiver can also be asked, "What are you most worried might happen next?" That question often surfaces risk more clearly than broad discussion of diagnosis, especially when the family has become accustomed to minimizing the seriousness of the situation.

It is equally important to ask questions that assess safety without sounding alarmist. “Has anyone talked about hurting themselves or someone else?” “Has there been any attempt to act on the belief?” “Are there weapons, substances, or other means that could increase danger?” “Has anyone refused essential medical care because of the belief?” “Has the person been sleeping, eating, or functioning normally?” These questions are not limited to crisis situations; they are part of understanding whether the shared belief is beginning to drive behavior in ways that could cause harm. In some cases, the most urgent concern is not direct violence but escalating loss of judgment, medical neglect, or a narrowing of the relationship so severe that no outside help can reach the people involved [7][4].

Finally, the most effective questions usually leave room for ambivalence. “What part of this feels certain, and what part feels confusing?” “What would need to happen for you to reconsider?” “What helps you feel safer without making things worse?” “Who could you talk to if you wanted another perspective?” “What kind of help would feel acceptable right now?” These questions respect the person’s current position while gently testing the flexibility of the belief and the openness of the relationship. In shared psychotic disorder, even small signs of doubt, distance, or curiosity can matter. A good conversation does not force immediate insight; it creates enough psychological space for insight to become possible.

Glossary of essential terms and concepts

A glossary in a text like this is not merely a convenience. It helps keep the clinical language stable when the same words can carry different meanings in ordinary conversation, in psychiatry, and in family life. Some terms describe symptoms, some describe relationship patterns, and some describe the practical realities that shape assessment and care. Because shared psychotic disorder is so closely tied to context, a reader may encounter the same concept in more than one setting and need a clear anchor for what it means here.

Delusion refers to a fixed false belief held with strong conviction despite clear evidence to the contrary. In this book, the term is used in its clinical sense, not as a casual way of describing stubbornness, misunderstanding, or disagreement. A delusion is not simply an unusual opinion; it is a belief that remains resistant to correction even when the person is presented with facts that would ordinarily change a reasonable conclusion.

Shared psychotic disorder is the term historically used for a condition in which a delusional belief develops in one person and is adopted by another person in the context of a close relationship. The central feature is not just similarity of belief, but the relational process through which the belief is sustained, reinforced, and made more compelling. Related terms you may see in the literature include folie à deux, shared psychosis, and shared delusional disorder [1][6][4].

Primary person and secondary person are practical labels used to describe the relative roles within the shared belief system. The primary person is typically the one whose delusional framework appears first or is most established, while the secondary person is the one who comes to share that belief. These terms are descriptive, not moral judgments, and they do not by themselves explain why the belief developed or which person is "more ill."

Inducer and recipient are older terms sometimes used in case reports and historical descriptions. They point to the same basic pattern: one person's conviction influences another's. In practice, however, the relationship is rarely so one-directional that it can be understood as simple transmission. The secondary person is not a passive container; susceptibility, dependency, fear, and reinforcement all shape what is adopted and what persists.

Reality testing is the capacity to compare an internal thought, fear, or interpretation with external evidence and to revise that interpretation when the facts do not support it. When reality testing is intact, a person can entertain uncertainty, consider alternatives, and tolerate disagreement. In shared psychotic disorder, reality testing may become narrowed around the shared belief, especially when the relationship itself discourages doubt or outside feedback.

Insight means awareness that one's beliefs, perceptions, or experiences may be part of an illness or may not accurately reflect reality. Insight is often partial rather than all-or-nothing. A person may recognize that others are concerned, yet still feel unable to question the belief itself. In shared psychotic disorder, insight can shift gradually, and it may improve first in one person before the other begins to reconsider the shared framework.

Enmeshment describes a relationship pattern in which personal boundaries are overly blurred and the emotional state of one person is tightly tied to the other. In enmeshed relationships, disagreement may feel like abandonment, and closeness may depend on maintaining the same interpretation of events. This does not cause shared psychosis on its own, but it can make a delusional belief harder to challenge because the relationship and the belief become intertwined.

Suggestibility is a heightened tendency to accept another person's interpretation, especially when that person is trusted, dominant, or emotionally central. It is not the same as weakness or naivety. Suggestibility becomes clinically important when it allows unusual explanations to gain authority before they have been carefully examined. Reinforcement refers to the repeated responses—verbal, emotional, or behavioral—that make the belief feel confirmed. Together, suggestibility and reinforcement can create a loop in which the belief gains strength simply by being repeated and protected.

Collateral information means information gathered from people or records outside the immediate interview, such as family members, prior clinicians, school reports, or medical documentation. In suspected shared psychotic disorder, collateral sources are often essential because the people directly involved may describe the situation in a way that reflects loyalty, fear, or the shared belief itself. Collateral information does not replace the patient's account; it helps place that account in context.

Differential diagnosis is the process of distinguishing one condition from others that can look similar. In this setting, it includes considering primary psychotic disorders, mood disorders with psychotic features, substance-related conditions, medical causes, trauma-related symptoms, and relational patterns that may resemble psychosis without meeting the full picture. Careful differential diagnosis matters because the treatment plan depends on what is actually driving the symptoms, not only on how dramatic the shared belief appears.

Comorbidity means the presence of more than one condition at the same time. Shared psychotic disorder often appears alongside anxiety, depression, trauma symptoms, insomnia, substance use, or another psychotic condition. Comorbidity can complicate the clinical picture because one problem may intensify another, and improvement in one area may not be enough if the rest of the system remains unchanged.

Safety planning is the process of identifying immediate risks and making a concrete plan to reduce harm. In shared psychotic disorder, this may involve limiting access to weapons, reducing exposure to escalating conflict, arranging emergency evaluation, or creating steps for what to do if the belief leads to self-harm, medical refusal, or aggression. Safety planning is not the same as solving the underlying problem; it is the first protection while assessment and treatment are underway.

Validation means acknowledging a person's emotions or distress without affirming the false belief as fact. For example, a caregiver can recognize fear, anger, or confusion without agreeing that the feared event is real. This distinction is central in family guidance because it allows support to remain compassionate without becoming part of the delusional system.

Relapse refers to the return or strengthening of symptoms after a period of improvement. In shared psychotic disorder, relapse may begin with renewed isolation, renewed contact with the reinforcing relationship, or a fresh stressor that narrows judgment. Protective factors are conditions that reduce risk or improve resilience, such as broader social contact, stable routines, treatment engagement, and relationships that encourage independent reality testing.

Resource list for crisis, treatment, and support services

When a crisis is unfolding, the first task is not to decide who is "right" about the belief, but to find the fastest path to safety, assessment, and appropriate care. In shared psychotic disorder, that often means knowing where to turn before the situation becomes more dangerous. Emergency departments, mobile crisis teams, psychiatric urgent care clinics, and local behavioral health hotlines can help when there is immediate risk of self-harm, aggression, severe neglect, or an inability to care for basic needs. If the person is in imminent danger or cannot remain safe, emergency services should be contacted right away. In the United States, calling or texting 988 connects to the Suicide & Crisis Lifeline, which can provide immediate support and help locate local resources. If there is an active emergency, calling 911 is appropriate.

For people who are already connected to outpatient care, the most useful treatment resources are often the ones that can respond quickly and coordinate across settings. A primary care clinician may help rule out medical contributors, but psychiatric evaluation is usually needed when fixed false beliefs are driving behavior. Community mental health centers, county behavioral health programs, and hospital-based outpatient psychiatry services may offer assessment, medication management, therapy, and case coordination. If the person's symptoms are severe, ask whether the program has experience with psychosis, family involvement, and crisis stabilization. When a relationship is highly enmeshed, it can also be helpful to ask whether separate appointments can be arranged so each person can speak freely without pressure from the other.

Families and caregivers often need support that is not limited to the person with the delusion. Psychoeducation, family therapy, and caregiver support groups can help reduce fear and prevent unhelpful responses that intensify conflict. NAMI, the National Alliance on Mental Illness, offers education programs, local support groups, and family resources in many communities. Mental Health America also provides screening tools, educational materials, and links to local services. For caregivers who are dealing with refusal of care, escalating suspicion, or repeated crisis episodes, a clinician or case manager can sometimes help connect the family to a higher level of support, such as intensive outpatient treatment, partial hospitalization, or assertive community treatment where available.

When the situation has become unstable, it is important to look for services that can address both psychiatric symptoms and the practical consequences of the disorder. Some people need help with sleep, medication adherence, substance use, housing, transportation, or protection from coercive relationships. Hospital social workers, community case managers, domestic violence advocates, adult protective services, and legal aid organizations may all become relevant depending on the circumstances. If the shared belief is occurring in a context of control, intimidation, or isolation, domestic violence hotlines and shelters can offer planning and safety options even when the person does not identify the relationship as abusive. If children, older adults, or vulnerable adults are being affected, protective services may need to be involved.

It can be useful to keep a short, local resource list prepared before a crisis peaks. Include the nearest emergency department with psychiatric services, the local crisis line, the outpatient psychiatrist or therapist, the primary care office, and the names and numbers of trusted family members or friends who can help with transportation or supervision. If the person has a history of psychosis, mania, severe depression, or prior hospitalization, keep those records and medication lists accessible. In a crisis, the ability to give a clear history can save time and reduce confusion. Because shared psychotic disorder often develops inside private relationships, outside helpers may not immediately understand the full pattern unless the information is organized and concise.

For readers who are seeking ongoing education or referral pathways, professional organizations can also be useful. The American Psychiatric Association, the American Psychological Association, and local psychiatric societies may provide directories, continuing education, and links to specialty care. University-affiliated psychiatric clinics can be especially helpful when the presentation is complex, diagnostically uncertain, or complicated by trauma, substance use, or medical illness. If a local clinician is unfamiliar with shared psychotic disorder, it may help to ask for referral to a psychiatrist, psychologist, or social worker with experience in psychosis-spectrum conditions. Case reports continue to show that the condition may present in emergency or family settings and can require coordinated medical and psychiatric attention [7][9][4].

Online information can be helpful, but it should be used cautiously. Reliable sources are those associated with recognized medical organizations, hospitals, universities, and public health agencies. Avoid websites that encourage confrontation, reinforce the delusion, or promise quick cures. In particular, any resource that urges secrecy, extreme isolation, or immediate dramatic action without professional oversight should be treated carefully. For a condition that is already shaped by narrowed reality and intense interpersonal pressure, the safest support is usually grounded, practical, and connected to real-world care.

www.ingramcontent.com/pod-product-compliance
Lightning Source LLC
LaVergne TN
LVHW100317210926
848480LV00003B/1163